Comments on other *Amazing Stories* from readers & reviewers

*"Tightly written volumes filled with lots of wit and humour
about famous and infamous Canadians."*
Eric Shackleton, *The Globe and Mail*

*"The heightened sense of drama and intrigue, combined with a
good dose of human interest is what sets* Amazing Stories *apart."*
Pamela Klaffke, *Calgary Herald*

*"This is popular history as it should be... For this price,
buy two and give one to a friend."*
Terry Cook, a reader from Ottawa, on **Rebel Women**

*"Glasner creates the moment of the explosion itself in
graphic detail...she builds detail upon gruesome detail
to create a convincingly authentic picture."*
Peggy McKinnon, *The Sunday Herald*, on **The Halifax Explosion**

*"It was wonderful...I found I could not put it down.
I was sorry when it was completed."*
Dorothy F. from Manitoba on **Marie-Anne Lagimodière**

*"Stories are rich in description, and bristle
with a clever, stylish realness."*
Mark Weber, *Central Alberta Advisor*, on **Ghost Town Stories II**

*"A compelling read. Bertin...has selected only the most intriguing
tales, which she narrates with a wealth of detail."*
Joyce Glasner, *New Brunswick Reader*, on **Strange Events**

*"The resulting book is one readers will want to share
with all the women in their lives."*
Lynn Martel, *Rocky Mountain Outlook*, on **Women Explorers**

LUCY MAUD
MONTGOMERY

LUCY MAUD MONTGOMERY

The Incredible Life of the
Creator of Anne of Green Gables

BIOGRAPHY

by Stan Sauerwein

PUBLISHED BY ALTITUDE PUBLISHING CANADA LTD.
1500 Railway Avenue, Canmore, Alberta T1W 1P6
www.altitudepublishing.com
1-800-957-6888

Extreme care has been taken to ensure that all information presented in
this book is accurate and up to date. Neither the author nor the
publisher can be held responsible for any errors.

Publisher	Stephen Hutchings
Associate Publisher	Kara Turner
Series Editor	Jill Foran
Editor	Lori Burwash
Digital Photo Colouring	Bryan Pezzi

We acknowledge the financial support of the Government
of Canada through the Book Publishing Industry Development
Program (BPIDP) for our publishing activities.

Altitude GreenTree Program
Altitude Publishing will plant twice as many trees as were used
in the manufacturing of this product.

We acknowledge the support of the Canada Council for the Arts which
in 2003 invested $21.7 million in writing and publishing throughout Canada.

 Canada Council   Conseil des Arts
for the Arts   du Canada

National Library of Canada Cataloguing in Publication Data

Sauerwein, Stan, 1952-
Lucy Maud Montgomery / Stan Sauerwein.

(Amazing stories)
Includes bibliographical references.
ISBN 1-55153-775-3

1. Montgomery, L. M. (Lucy Maud), 1874-1942. 2. Novelists,
Canadian (English)--20th century--Biography. I. Title.
II. Series: Amazing stories (Canmore, Alta.)

PS8526.O55Z874 2004   C813'.52   C2004-902706-9

Printed and bound in Canada by Friesens
2 4 6 8 9 7 5 3

To the writer in all of us

Lucy Maud Montgomery at the time of
publication of *Anne of Green Gables*, 1908.

Contents

Prologue

Maud sorted through her papers and dejectedly separated the letters of rejection. It hardly seemed fair that the last one had been so blunt, but she shrugged it off. "After all," she told herself, "you are only starting to find your own voice as a writer."

True to the schedule she was trying to maintain every day, Maud had gotten up that morning before dawn to steal some time for her passion — writing. Her grandmother was still asleep, the stove was stoked for breakfast, and any other household chores could wait a few hours.

Maud opened her small black notebook and began to leaf through it page by page, looking for an idea. Her fast scrawl, developing into a personal kind of shorthand, covered the sheets in careful scratches. They were glimpses of her moods, random thoughts, and dreamy passages with snippets of prose.

As she scanned, however, the last rejection letter for her secretly written novel pestered her. She'd put so much time into it. Surely some of it was salvageable. Perhaps a shortened version might be accepted for a Sunday school paper. I can earn $5 for that, and heaven knows I need the money, she thought.

Petting her cat, Maud tried to remember what she had

done with the manuscript. She searched through the stacks on her writing desk and then suddenly remembered. The hatbox!

Maud pulled the box from the cupboard and scooped out her handwritten pages. With a satisfied murmur, she made herself comfortable at her desk and began to read. She hadn't got through half the manuscript when she decided her character deserved one more chance.

"It's really not half bad," Maud whispered to herself. She stuffed the pages into an envelope and gave it a gentle pat. "Good luck, Anne with an 'e.'"

Chapter 1
Charity Case

She was born under a dark star and destined to walk a hard path.

Lucy Maud Montgomery entered the world on festive St. Andrew's Day, November 30, 1874, but those celebrations did not foretell a life of happiness.

She was born after a hard labour in a modest frame house, pretentiously named Clifton House, that overlooked that tiny Prince Edward Island (PEI) village's harbour. The only child conceived by Hugh John Montgomery and Clara Woolner Macneill, she was reverently named Lucy after her Grandmother Macneill and Maud in honour of Queen Victoria's daughter. She would grow to dislike the name Lucy, preferring Maud instead. Using it for most of her life, Maud was always insistent it be spelled properly — *without* the 'e.'

At 33, Hugh was worldly. Once a captain in the merchant marine, he'd sailed to exotic ports in South America and the West Indies, far from the red sandstone cliffs of their island in the Gulf of St. Lawrence. He'd been a success at that freewheeling life, but in Clifton, the son of PEI's first senator didn't fare so well. He struggled to earn his living while ashore, trying to squeeze profit from a failing general store.

Just a year before "Maudie" was born to the couple, PEI had become the Canadian Confederation's newest province. The dream of a nation spreading far to the west fuelled the imaginations of men like Hugh. Based on news from a few friends who'd moved to a strange-sounding place called Saskatchewan, Hugh contemplated that dream. Better business opportunities, he believed, awaited men of courage and vision in Canada's Northwest Territories. Anything would be better than Clifton, where his business opportunities were slim. But he now had a wife and child to support, and besides, Clara was not well enough to travel.

Maud's mother was a pretty but frail girl of pioneering stock. The rustic island life could be hard on its women. Clara's health showed it. Within just 21 months of Maud's birth, Clara contracted tuberculosis. Unable to care for his wife and child while running the store, Hugh moved them to the isolated north coast hamlet of Cavendish (then known as Cawnpore), 38 kilometres from the nearest railroad station, and put them in the care of Clara's mother on the family homestead.

Soon after the family arrived in Cavendish, Clara's disease worsened to a case of "galloping consumption." Her decline was steady and swift. On September 1, 1876, she passed away, just 23 years old.

Her mother's death transformed little Lucy Maud into a kind of orphan, even though her father was alive and she belonged to a huge clan of relatives. Maud had 35 first cousins on PEI alone. Two hundred people lived in her maternal grandparents' village, and half of them were family. The Macneills, the Simpsons, and the Clarks were all original settlers of the area. The branches of Maud's extended family had intermarried so often, a complex web of familial relationships had been created among most residents of Cavendish. Among her relatives were poets, storytellers, politicians, farmers, and elders of the Presbyterian Church. They all turned up for Clara's funeral, an event that became Maud's earliest memory.

Maud had been held in her weeping father's arms and shown Clara's lifeless body. She remembered it all clearly for the rest of her life. She remembered how the cold flesh of her mother's thin face felt to her tiny hand. She remembered how the sunlight streamed through the parlour window to create leafy shadows on the floor, and how, even at her young age, she understood that she'd lost a very important person.

Needing constant care, which was something her father obviously couldn't provide, baby Maud was left with her maternal grandparents in Cavendish. In their late 50s, the

Macneills had already raised six children. They were hardly the best candidates to rear an energetic little girl, but they accepted the family obligation grudgingly. Alexander Macneill was both a farmer and orchardist and served his community as the postmaster. He was stern, domineering, and irritable. Lucy Macneill was cold, reserved, and narrow in her affections. Still, in their own way, they loved Maud and folded her into their lives as an inconvenience to be endured.

Maud learned early to make do. She was given a tiny room on the upper floor of the Macneills' home with a window that faced west toward the farm's hills and woods. From "the lookout," she enjoyed pretend games of make-believe with used dolls. While she missed her mother and father, the room was cozy and she had her "babies" for company. Never mind that one had a broken head and the other a missing arm. Maud overlooked their infirmities. Imperfect as they were, the dolls were her playmates. In fact, until Maud was old enough for school, the dolls and the cats roaming the barnyard were her only real friends.

Maud's time with her grandparents was more an imprisonment than a reprieve from her grief. As strict Presbyterians, the Macneills disapproved of fanciful enjoyments. They didn't celebrate birthdays. Singing in the household was a rarity. When it happened, the melodies were restricted to hymns. As Maud grew up, evenings after supper were usually spent with Alexander reading from the Bible. Perhaps because of it, Maud caught on to the reading habit early. By the time she was four, she'd taught herself to read and had already devoured her *Royal Reader* repeatedly before graduating to "acceptable" novels and poems she was allowed to read any day but Sunday.

For a child, life with the Macneills was lonely. Though Maud's grandparents maintained a social connection with the rest of Cavendish, guests in the Macneill household were usually limited to relatives. As boring as their visits were to a little girl, at least they were occasions when Grandfather Macneill came out of his irascible shell for a few brief hours, and young Lucy Maud learned to look forward to them. While he may have been too deaf to carry on a conversation, Alexander could spin entertaining stories and did it often during those visits. Though Maud feared the old man with his scowling demeanour, his entertainments planted another seed in the young girl. This one for storytelling.

In those early years at Cavendish, Maud's father was a regular visitor to the farm. Until Maud was old enough for school, Hugh would arrive with smiles and hugs and bundle her off for beach walks and long buggy rides in the countryside. Maud relished that time. She basked in her father's affection because, between his stopovers, all she felt was the constant assault of her grandfather's ill will and the cool indifference of her grandmother. Overt shows of affection were alien in the stern Macneill household.

With her father's business failing, Hugh was unable to contribute much toward Maud's upkeep. Alexander's complaints about the cost of her upbringing, without what he considered to be adequate contribution, built resentments in the little girl. She was also often the brunt of teasing when cousins came to visit. Between her cousins' persecution, her Aunt Ann Maria's scorn, and her Uncle John's bullying, Maud's resentment increased. She felt that the pain she had to endure was unfair. When settling squabbles between Maud and her cousins, Lucy Macneill would rarely rise to her granddaughter's defence in the same protective way her aunt did for her children. Motherless Maud felt those slaps to her spirit particularly hard. She came to feel her family, including her grandparents, considered her a "charity case." The implied inadequacy crippled Maud's self-esteem.

However, the Macneills' attitude also stoked an anger in Maud and a need to prove herself. She developed a fierce independence and steely core of will. Even so, she continued to feel she was a hapless victim of circumstance. "It's a great misfortune for a child to be brought up by old people," she later observed sadly. Maud loved her grandparents, but as an adult she qualified that affection. "In material respects [my grandparents] were good and kind to me and I am sincerely grateful to them, but in many respects they were unwise in their treatment of me."

Being a lonely child among older adults fired Maud's imagination. Two decades later, she wrote about how her isolation had shaped her creatively: "I was shut out from all social life, even such as this small country settlement could offer, debarred from the companionship of other children, and in early youth, other young people. I had not companionship except that of books and solitary rambles in wood and fields. This drove me in on myself and early forced me to construct for myself a world of fancy and imagination very different indeed from the world in which I lived."

Maud's fantasy world included playmates besides her dolls and cats. In the glass doors of a cabinet in her grandmother's parlour, Maud conjured two imaginary friends with whom she would often chat. In the left-hand door was Katie Maurice, a girl her own age; in the right-hand door was Lucy Gray, a widowed woman. Maud preferred to spend time with Katie, but never neglected to bring lonely Lucy Gray into her conversations.

Despite Maud's sense of isolation, she had many relatives who did treat her with love and affection. Her Aunt Emily, the youngest of the Macneill daughters, was warm and loving toward Maud and became almost a surrogate mother to the girl. Senator Donald and Mrs. Montgomery opened their hearts to their skinny and precocious granddaughter as well. And her father's kin, the Campbells, who lived near the Montgomery farm in Park Corner, 20 kilometres from Cavendish, always welcomed her into their midst. Maud's aunt Annie Macneill, who had married John Campbell, treated Maud as just another of the children they had scrambling about their rambling home.

Maud loved her visits to Park Corner, a day's journey

The Green Gables National Historic site in Cavendish,
PEI. Lucy Maud used to visit this house, and it
became the inspiration for her Anne stories.

by buggy from the Macneill homestead. She loved "the jolly racket" in the house the Campbells called Silver Bush. Of the nine children born to her aunt and uncle, only five had survived, but each was like a sibling to Maud. Her strongest bond was with a trio of cousins: Clara, Stella, and Fredericka. There was "so much laughter at Silver Bush," Maud later recalled, "that the very walls seemed soaked in it."

Maud and her Campbell cousins roamed the land around Silver Bush on a constant hunt for fun. They fished the brooks, picked berries, and explored the nooks and crannies in the Campbell home with happy abandon. For Maud, the time at Silver Bush was especially delicious without the ever-present fear of a harsh word from Alexander or Lucy's criticism to curb her delight. "I have never heard anything sweeter than the whistling of the robins at sunset in the maple woods around those fields," she later wrote. It was such a dear memory that Maud used Silver Bush as the setting for one of the novels that would make her and PEI famous.

In contrast to the high times at Silver Bush, Maud's life in Cavendish was generally tedious. It was definitely not always pleasant. She grew to fear her grandfather and his humiliations and to bridle at her grandmother's terse words. She turned, first subconsciously and later consciously, away from the strictures of the Presbyterian faith her grandparents rigidly enforced. Instead of remembering the joys of prayer, she later described feelings of "anger, humiliation and disgust" at being forced to kneel on the floor and pray for God's forgiveness because she had been a bad girl. "Something inside me was outraged ... To force a human soul to utter words of prayer and contrition when not in a fit state to do so — when stormy rebellion and bitterness filled it!"

The episode left her with a dislike for displays of public praying and religion in general. It caused a feeling in her that lurked "under all the beliefs and conclusions of my reason — that religion and all connected with it was something which — like sex — it is necessary to have but made one feel ashamed for all that."

A travelling preacher with the Bible Society who visited the Macneill home twice a year didn't help matters. He repelled the young Maud physically, and she never forgot her observations of him or how she felt when he once asked, "Little girl, isn't it nice to be a Christian?" To Maud, if he represented what it meant to be a Christian, she didn't wish to be one. He was thin and pale and had a scraggly beard and squeaky voice. She noted his "shivery bony form, pinched blue face, purple hands." For the rest of her life, she was never quite able to separate her memory of him from her idea of Christianity.

Instead, Maud's faith departed from the norm to something more personally spiritual, demonstrated as a love of nature. She kept her religious rebellion secret her whole life. Turning inward, she found a kind of religious solace in the playful attention of her feline playmates and the constancy of the seasons as she rambled alone in the countryside.

To Maud, the woods, orchards, and beaches around her Cavendish home were magical. "Everything," she wrote, "was invested with a kind of fairy grace and charm, emanating from my own fancy, the trees that whispered nightly around the old house where I slept, the woodsy nooks I explored, the homestead fields, each individualized by some oddity or fence or shape, the sea whose murmur was never out of my ears — all were radiant with 'the glory and the dream' ... amid all the commonplaces of life, I was very near to a kingdom of ideal beauty. Between it and me hung only a thin veil. I could never draw it quite aside, but sometimes a wind fluttered it and I caught a glimpse of the enchanting realm beyond — only a glimpse — but those glimpses have always made life worth while."

While Maud was growing up in the Macneill household, her father took on various occupations to replace the financial void caused when his general store finally went bankrupt. At one point, it appears he was involved with a company shipping produce across the country. He travelled away in summer but always returned in winter. Although he never left PEI for long, the business ventures evidently rekindled the thoughts he'd been harbouring for years about opportunity in Canada's westernmost territories.

Hugh finally made a decision to pursue those potentials in the spring of 1882 and informed Maud that he was going to Prince Albert, Saskatchewan. Though she had never seen her father on a daily basis, the news must have given Maud a fresh dose of abandonment. She'd grown up in a cocoon of isolation, her rare moments of freedom broken only by his visits. Though her grandparents were kind enough to take her in, they never failed to remind Maud of their sacrifice, or that she was at the receiving end of a Christian charity and, because of it, was less worthy.

Now her father was leaving without her. It dashed Maud's hope that one day she and he would share a home of their own, a place where she wouldn't feel like she was imposing on a relative's kindness. But she had no choice in the matter. This was to be the way of things and she accepted her situation sadly.

Fortunately her father's departure coincided with a time when Maud's world was expanding. By then she was attending the one-room school across the road from her grandparents' farm, and with that came new challenges.

Chapter 2
A Taste of Freedom

aud's first day in school had started wonderfully. Aunt Emily helped Maud with her shiny new button-down boots. She carefully adjusted the girl's hat atop her waist-length tresses and tugged the creases from her freshly ironed pinafore. She even walked Maud, hand in hand, through the gate at the bottom of the Macneills' farmyard and across the road to a new world, a world of wonder and words, filled with the expectation of friendships and fun.

From there, however, things became decidedly less wonderful as the sheltered young girl quickly discovered that her grandparents' view of the world differed from the rest of Cavendish. Maud entered the school with her hat firmly

planted and was immediately adopted by some older classmates and seated with them. The older children traditionally
guided new students in the decorum of school life. However,
they didn't tell Maud everything.

Having left her hat on through the first session of classes,
Maud clearly stood out. Wearing high-button shoes when all
the other pupils went barefoot was another strike against her.
"Miss Pridey, Miss Pridey, you may have button boots, but
you are living on charity," the children teased. Her pinafore,
a long sacklike dress, also drew raucous bouts of teasing during her first recess period. The boys called it a "baby apron."
Maud's embarrassment over her attire ran deep. "I felt that I
was a target for the humiliation of the universe. Never, I felt
certain, could I live down such a terrible mistake."

To make matters worse, because the Macneills' farm
was so close to the school, her grandmother insisted Maud
return home for a hot lunch every day. Children who lived
farther away were able to spend their noon hours socializing.
But her grandmother's command meant that Maud couldn't
expand her circle of friends. That too gave Maud reason to
resent life in Cavendish.

For several months Maud endured the schoolyard teasing about her clothes, which was remarkable considering that
she'd developed a hot temper. But Maud had an agile mind.
Compared to her classmates, she was well read. Growing up
with her grandfather's incessant sarcasm, she was also well-
armed with verbal assaults. When she'd finally had enough of

the teasing, Maud lashed back with stinging comments of her own. Before long, her classmates figured out that teasing the long-haired girl was always a mistake, and they avoided her.

Not everybody backed away though. Maud had built a friendship with her cousin Penzie Macneill, three years her senior, and another cousin, Lucy. Maud's grandmother even finally allowed Penzie to visit Maud after school in the Macneill home, a privilege no one else at school was accorded by her grandmother.

In the summer of 1883, Maud had other companions join her state of confinement at the Macneill homestead. At the start of her second year of school, two brothers, Wellington and David Nelson, became boarders in her home. Orphans, the Nelson boys were being cared for by their aunt. Because they lived too far from school for daily travel, their aunt paid the Macneills to take them in for three school years.

In Maud's eyes, the boys were a delight. Energetic, hot-tempered, and wild, they were a ready source of fun and new experiences. "Well" was eight years old, and "Dave" was seven, perfect ages for eight-year-old Maud. Their battling offered her no end of entertainment, and she happily joined them fishing in the brooks on the farm or building play forts in the woods. Thanks to the Nelson brothers, Maud remembered those girlhood years with great fondness.

Maud's other friends on the farm were of course the cats. Whenever she accompanied the boys on their outdoor adventures, she would bring one kitten or another, often tucked safely in her apron. Her favourites were Pussy-willow and Catkin. But when Maud was nine, she experienced the grief of death for the second time with the death of Pussy-willow.

Maud's grandmother refused to allow the barn cats into the house. So when the Macneills' dog, Gyp, had been harassing Pussy-willow to distraction, Maud locked the cat in the barn to give her some peace. When she returned to release her, Maud was shocked to encounter her pet suffering a painful death. Maud didn't know the barn had been baited with rat poison. The cat had apparently found a rat and eaten her fill of the poisoned carcass.

Bundling the suffering animal in her arms, Maud helplessly stroked her as she watched her life ebb. When the cat died, it "... was the first time anything I really loved left me forever," she later wrote. Despite the trauma of her mother's passing, the death of Pussy-willow gave her the most grief. Even 25 years later, Maud still mourned her friend, believing the death was her fault. "The scar of that hurt is still on my soul," she wrote.

Maud's ninth year was momentous for other reasons, too.

School had helped Maud realize she had a deep desire to write and an inherent expressive talent. She looked at the world in a unique way, as an artist might appreciate colours and tones. The way she saw things bolstered her poetic nature, and she actively attempted to express herself in verse.

Poetry was, for her, the closest approximation to painting. Maud wanted to create images with words the way an artist did on canvas, and she hoped to someday emulate great poets such as Byron and Shelley. She knew in her heart that she had a talent with words, and she ached to share her gift with others.

Maud's first attempt was inspired by James Thomson's "The Seasons." She wrote her poem in free verse and titled it "Autumn." Not surprisingly, it described the changing colours of the lands around Cavendish: "Now autumn comes, laden with peach and pear; / The sportsman's horn is heard throughout the land, / And the poor partridge, fluttering, falls dead."

She waited patiently for an opportunity to show the poem to somebody. Her first chance for a sympathetic ear came when her father returned to Cavendish for a visit.

In a quiet moment, she proudly approached him.

Hugh read the poem and passed it back, evidently unimpressed.

"It's blank verse," said Maud, showing him her knowledge on the subject.

"Very blank," her father replied.

The reaction devastated the young poet but it didn't stop her from writing. Over the next three years, she accumulated more poems and a few short stories, which she wrote on the back of post office "letter bills" her grandfather discarded three times a week.

At the age of 12, Maud carefully copied one of those poems into presentable form and made her first submission to a magazine. It was promptly rejected, which chilled her publishing passion for a year before she had the courage to submit another poem to the Charlottetown *Examiner*. It, like the first poem, was rejected, but Maud still felt the fledgling writer's hope of recognition.

Resolving not to give up, Maud began practising her vocabulary in everyday conversation around Cavendish. These attempts to improve herself were met with uncomplimentary laughter from the adults in the village. To many, the language was far too sophisticated for a young child, especially coming from a girl.

While she didn't let the jeering discourage her from pursuing her dream of being a writer, Maud's self-conscious nature did take over. She wrote her poems and stories in secret from then on and used the convenience of having the post office in her grandfather's home to cover her activity. She sent manuscript after manuscript out to the world from that kitchen post office and watched as manuscript after manuscript was returned, rejected. She continued anyway, creating stories and poems of all kinds, from tragic odes of death to fanciful tales of fairies. For practice, she even rewrote her favourite novels, changing the plots to put the heroines in control of their destiny.

Soon after her 12th birthday, Maud received news from her father that was both exciting and alarming. He was getting remarried. While in Prince Albert, Hugh had met the attractive stepdaughter of railway magnate William McKenzie, a friend of Hugh's father. Mary Ann McRae was a strikingly lovely young woman only 12 years older than Maud.

This happy news spawned doubts for Maud. Would this new mother grow to love her? Would she be forgotten by her father, who would no doubt be occupied with duties of setting up a new household?

In April 1887, Hugh married Mary Ann. Maud initiated a devoted letter-writing campaign to Mary Ann, attempting to open a line of communication and generate a friendship with her new mother. Offering Mary Ann detailed descriptions of life in Cavendish, Maud painted her word pictures of its rustic beauty and even enclosed pressed wildflowers in the letters. But Maud, much to her dismay, received no assurances from Mary Ann that she would be welcomed into her father's new family.

As Maud had expected, her father was busy establishing himself in Prince Albert. In his first three years there, he'd been a land agent, an auctioneer, and a forest ranger. Though two of his businesses suffered the same fate as his store in Clifton, Hugh had managed to make enough money to build himself a house. (He also managed to be accused of defrauding two men.)

In the meantime, Maud waited, hopeful that one day her father would send for her. To fill her time, she focussed on her school work and her writing.

Finally, the summer before she turned 16, Maud's dream of living with her father came true. Accompanying her grandfather Montgomery on a momentous journey across the country, Maud set out to join Hugh and at last meet her stepmother.

Chapter 3
Prince Albert
Adventures

hen Maud left PEI with her grandfather, she felt she was launching on an adventure. The trip represented a fresh chapter in her life, but it also promised to provide grist for more stories. Maud sincerely believed that one day she would be a successful writer. She practised daily the discipline of her craft. The diary she had begun at the age of nine was already taking the more sophisticated form of a journal. In it, she recorded ideas for future writing projects and snippets of poems and had begun confessing her deeper, more secret longings.

The journey west had an auspicious start. Donald had arranged for Maud and himself to travel to Summerside, PEI, aboard a train carrying Canadian prime minister Sir John. A. Macdonald and his wife on a tour through the province. Six days after leaving Prince Edward Island, at 5:00 a.m. on a foggy morning, Maud and her grandfather reached Regina. Maud had a tearful reunion with her father, and the next day the trio boarded a freight train on a branch line. They took their "caboose" ride as far as the line would go and finished the 320-kilometre journey to Prince Albert on a buckboard.

The city was pleasant enough to Maud, set in a valley high above sea level and surrounded by forests, lakes, and bluffs. But, having been incorporated only five years earlier, Prince Albert was booming and new. Maud found herself homesick for quaint Cavendish.

Soon after their arrival, Donald left to continue his journey west and Hugh joined him nine days later. That left Maud alone with Mary Ann. She quickly discovered that she and Mary Ann shared a strong dislike for each other. Perhaps Mary Ann viewed Maud as a competitor for Hugh's affections in a marriage that was showing signs of strain. Whatever the reason, Maud's hope of finding a woman who would be the nurturing mother she'd never had was dashed. Instead, she encountered a domineering, demanding woman she immediately disliked.

Mary Ann echoed the same sentiments and demonstrated them in mean little ways. She refused to allow Maud to wear her hair up, for example, because it made Maud look more mature. "I don't want the women to think me old enough to have a grown up step-daughter," Mary Ann, just 27 herself, declared with irritation. Rather than permitting Maud the freedom to explore her new community or the luxury of living in a home with a maid, Mary Ann insisted Maud pitch in with the housework. It was far from the dream of domestic harmony Maud had wished for for so long.

The situation became so uncomfortable that soon after Hugh returned to Prince Albert, Maud gently complained about her treatment. Hugh confessed that even he often found Mary Ann hard to take, but he did nothing to enforce a truce between them.

Life in the frontier city got worse by the month. Mary Ann was usually at the heart of Maud's discomfort. She hated it when dinnertime stories drifted to a recounting of the old times in Cavendish. She raised loud objections if Hugh endearingly referred to his daughter as "Maudie." She had temper tantrums when she couldn't get her way with Hugh. If the tantrums still didn't get her what she wanted, she reverted to loud crying jags. She was constantly seeking to better her domestic surroundings with expensive purchases, and she railed at Hugh for not being able to afford more extravagances.

Maud, however, attempted to endure, playing the role of polite daughter, all the while keeping up with her writing. Just before her 16th birthday, she completed a 156-line poem about a murder at Cape Le Force, near Cavendish, and submitted it to the *Charlottetown Patriot*.

Like a birthday present a few weeks later, she received a copy of the November 26 edition. Her poem, all 39 verses, had been given a full column on the front page. "The moment we see our first darling brainchild arranged in black type is never to be forgotten. It has in it some of the wonderful awe and delight that comes to a mother when she looks for the first time on the face of her first born," Maud noted afterward. "It was the first sweet bubble on the cup of success and of course it intoxicated me."

When school opened for a new term in September 1890, Maud was relieved to join the other 16 pupils, if only to escape the burden of housework. The Prince Albert school was far different from the one-room institution Maud had grown up with in Cavendish. Its rooms served all sorts of double duty. The classroom where she was taught functioned as the ladies' area for the dance hall upstairs at night. The building hosted the Prince Albert city council meetings, and the North-West Mounted Police maintained a cellblock in the building as well.

Maud and Annie McTaggart were the only girls attending the school when Maud arrived. The school, a multi-storeyed warren of rooms that would later become a hotel, was a microcosm of the wild and woolly frontier community. The student population reflected that. The heavy skew to males in her class showed itself plainly in the schoolmaster's style of teaching and discipline. John Mustard, a young man himself at 22, used violence or the threat of it to maintain order. A lazy, bad-tempered instructor, he would wield a raw-hide whip on disobedient pupils, sometimes in self-defence.

Annie became a good friend of Maud's, but it was her neighbour, Laura Pritchard, who made life in Prince Albert bearable. Laura attended St. Anne's Convent, along with most girls in Prince Albert, but she spent all her free time at Maud's side. The girls were inseparable. "I never met a girl I could confide in as I can Laura," Maud wrote. "I can tell her everything — the thoughts of my very inmost soul — and she is the same with me. We are twin spirits in every way."

Although Maud was happy in her schooling and her friendship with Laura, Mary Ann had other plans for her stepdaughter. In January 1891, she gave birth to Hugh's second child. Bruce was a colicky baby boy Maud soon came to dislike. Mary Ann ignored Maud's desire to finish school and instead, pressed her into service as a babysitter for the wailing child. When a string of maids fled Mary Ann's criticism-ridden employ, Maud also became the house servant. Dutiful to her father and feeling obligated to assist domestically, she took on both roles while Mary Ann socialized among Prince Albert's higher society.

Maud continued to write in her spare time, however. In February, she dusted off her notes and penned a poem titled *The Wreck of the Marco Polo*, which recounted the 1883 demise of what had once been the fastest sailing vessel of her class. After the ship sprang leaks, the captain ran her into the sandbanks offshore from Cavendish.

In order to help defray the loss of the vessel, the captain launched a two-week salvage operation. During this time, he stayed with the Macneills, regaling them with stories of the desperate measures he was forced to take to save his crew. Eight-year-old Maud, crouched under the kitchen table, had soaked it all up. When the salvage operation was done, Maud watched in amazement as the captain covered the kitchen table with a mountain of gold that was then parcelled out to the departing crew.

Maud had never forgotten her astonishment at seeing so much gold at one time, nor the incredible stories of the crew's close call with death. She submitted the 1600-word poem to the *Montreal Witness*. Told in a powerfully descriptive style that captured her recollections perfectly, the poem won Maud third prize for Queen's County in the Canada Prize Competition.

However, the fatigue brought on by long nights tending the baby and longer days doing housework began to wear Maud down physically. In March, she contracted a bad chest cold. Three months later, she was still coughing. She began to seriously resent the treatment she was getting. Nonetheless, she continued writing. Between bouts of housework and babysitting, Maud crafted the article "A Western Eden," about Prince Albert and Saskatchewan, and was encouraged one more time when it was published in the *Prince Albert Times*.

By this time, Maud was blossoming into an attractive young woman. Her hair was a dark, shiny curtain that fell to below her narrow waist. She had a pert mouth and aquiline nose. While her figure was far from the hourglass shape fashionable at the time, Maud had begun to show a penchant for fashion. She enjoyed wearing stylish clothes, including hats festooned with ostrich plumes, and adorning herself with inexpensive jewellery and accessories.

With that beauty came newfound attention. To that point in Maud's life, the advances of males had been restricted to childish attempts by schoolboys. The winter before she left for Prince Albert, she'd received her first love letter, from fellow student Nate Lockhart.

It had been a school superstition that if a girl counted nine stars for nine nights in a row, the first boy she shook hands with after that was destined to become her husband. In his letters, Nate confessed he'd accomplished the starry task and had also managed to shake hands with Maud. "When I read that it was I with whom he had shaken hands I nearly had a fit for I had never suspected that. But I forgot surprise and everything else when I saw that fatal question ... It was: 'Which of your boy friends do you like best?' Horrors! I had never dreamed of this!"

Unfortunately for Nate, the island girl had a purpose in her life — to write — and falling into the trap of early marriage was not in her cards. The more sentimental Nate's correspondence, the cooler she was toward him. She recorded her feelings in her journal. "I don't care a bit for Nate that way — I really don't. I only just like him splendidly as a chum.

I don't mean to take any further notice of his nonsense, yet I admit I do feel a queer, foolish triumphant little feeling about it. I've often wondered if anyone would ever care for me — that way — and now someone really has."

With one suitor's heart already broken, Maud soon found herself attracting the attention of a new admirer — John Mustard. Perhaps her publishing success gave her reason to carry herself differently. Perhaps she was just maturing. It might even have been possible that Mary Ann was encouraging the schoolteacher as a means of getting rid of Maud. For whatever reason, once Maud turned 16, John began to show an inordinate amount of interest in her.

With Mary Ann's consent, John began calling on Maud at home whenever Hugh was away, courting his student with obvious desires. Dealing remotely with a boy her own age was one thing, but facing a *man* pressing his case for romance was quite another. Maud was uncertain just how blunt she should be in discouraging John. It was obvious to her that they had very little in common. Conversations began with school and inevitably slipped to religion, a topic John must have felt Maud, coming from a Presbyterian family, would be interested in discussing.

It was the completely wrong tactic. Confiding to her journal, Maud referred to the slight and boring teacher as "that detestable Mustard." To protect herself from his advances, she began inviting Laura to her home when she suspected John might call. Even though she and Laura made jokes at the smitten man's expense, it didn't seem to dissuade him. No matter the weather, even in the face of blizzards, John continued to call. Maud's wooing became the talk of Prince Albert, likely thanks to Mary Ann's penchant for gossip.

On July 1, 1891, John finally stoked his courage for the question.

"I feel like shrieking ... I had what Laura calls 'a creepy, crawly presentiment,' that something was just on the point of happening. He looked out of the window while I glared at a piece of yellow yarn on the carpet ... and wished myself a thousand miles away. Finally Mr. Mustard turned with a very ghastly sort of smile and stammered out painfully, 'Do you think, Miss Montgomery, that our friendship will ever develop into anything else?' And his look and tone plainly revealed what he meant by 'anything else.' Well, I had to say something, so I said, 'I don't see what else it can develop into, Mr. Mustard.' I said it very well and composedly, too. I had expected to be flustered — but I wasn't ... 'It's just as you think,' he said slowly ... [H]e stammered out that he 'hoped I wasn't offended — he did not wish any misunderstanding' — This was my chance so I dashed in nobly and blurted out, 'Certainly not, Mr. Mustard. And I shall always be your friend but nothing more.' Then — silence! Oh, dear, it was really dreadful. And there were actually tears in his eyes. But I didn't cry or feel like crying. He has brought it all on himself, for any sane man might have taken the hint that I had no use for him long ago. I just wanted to laugh ... I am devoutly thankful that the dreaded ordeal is over."

While Maud was fending off John's advances, she noticed yet another suitor. Laura's brother, Will, was showing signs of interest in her. It was confirmed in an early morning conversation with Laura on a sleepover: "'Do you know,' whispered Laura, 'I believe Willy will just break his heart when you go away. Look here, I never say anything but I know this — he just worships the ground you tread on.' I laughed and said 'nonsense.' But I smiled a wee bit to myself in the darkness. It's nice to be — liked!" But Maud considered Will little more than a friend. "He just seems like a brother or a jolly good comrade to me," she recorded. Maud felt in many ways that Will was a kindred spirit, and she liked him well enough not to hurt his feelings with an overt rejection.

Amid all the suitors, Maud was receiving as many as eight letters a day from home while she was in Prince Albert. It was "dreadful to be among strangers all the time," she replied to friends. She repeatedly bemoaned the fact that she was desperately homesick for her beloved Cavendish. Finally, on August 27, 1891, her father gave in and sent Maud back to PEI.

The day before she left, Will pressed a letter into her hand and meekly asked her not to forget him. She recorded her reply in her journal: "'I'll never forget you, you may be sure,' I said, as we shook hands. 'Good-bye ...' Our hands fell apart and he was gone, I felt so badly I couldn't cry — I just felt stupid. I went up to my room and read his letter. He said in it that he loved me and always would. I curled up on my bed after I had read it and had a good cry. I felt so lonesome and horrid. If I hadn't known that Will had left town I believe I'd have run out after him."

The next day Maud began her homeward journey. It took 10 days to reach Cavendish and she arrived there during a storm. It was a synchronistic foreshadowing of what lay ahead.

Chapter 4
Back to School

Maud had grown up a good deal in her time away from Cavendish. Her successes with writing had bolstered her self-esteem, and she knew exactly what she wanted for the rest of her life. She wanted to complete her education, obtain a teacher's certificate, and, with a job, begin her writing career.

Unfortunately, Grandfather Macneill hadn't changed at all, besides becoming functionally deaf. When Maud re-entered life in Cavendish, she sat with him and laboriously tried to explain her dream. To her disappointment, the elderly man not only mocked her intentions, he flatly refused to help her achieve them. He called her plan frivolous. Without his financial support, Maud realized she'd have to try something other than a frontal assault on miserly Alexander.

That winter and into the early months of 1892, Maud spent most of her time in Park Corner giving her Campbell cousins, Clara, Stella, and George, organ lessons. By summer her grandfather relented. The Macneills agreed to put money together for her to attend teachers' college. To be accepted, however, Maud had to return to the Cavendish school for a final year and prepare for her entrance exams.

Maud attacked her studies with a vengeance. On her matriculation, she placed fifth in the province out of 264 graduating high school students. It was a satisfying accomplishment. Through the school term, Maud had to put up with both her grandfather's derisive predictions of failure and her grandmother's condescension for aspiring to something better than life as a farmer's wife. With the matriculation hurdle overcome, Maud took a buggy ride out of Cavendish and headed on her own to Prince of Wales College in Charlottetown. She was not yet 19.

While the Macneills and her father had scraped together enough money for Maud to attend college, there was very little to spare. She had to be judicious with every penny. To save on expenses, she boarded at a house, sharing a room with a third cousin, Mary Campbell.

The boarding house, owned by a tightfisted widow named Barbara MacMillan, presented Maud with a test of her will. The meals Mrs. MacMillan offered as part of her rent were small and foul, and Maud was constantly hungry. If it wasn't the quality of the meals, it was the lack of variety that turned her away from the widow's table. During one month, Maud was served boiled mutton for 21 dinners in a row.

When winter arrived, the trial got even worse. Mrs. MacMillan was miserly with the supply of coal to heat the house. Maud often had to cover her bed with all her clothes and floor mats in order to sleep. The conditions were nearly intolerable. In the February cold, Maud would wake to find ice crusting the water jug in her room.

Miraculously, she persisted and overcame the miserable odds. To graduate on the meagre funds available, Maud crowded the two-year curriculum into a single year. She studied for the college exams as if nothing else in life mattered. It was fortunate she did. The exams were so difficult only 9 out of 120 students in her class passed. Immediately afterward, she wrote her teaching licence examinations, placing fifth out of 18 applicants.

Once again Maud had proven her intelligence and determination. But although her grandfather had caved to her appeals to attend college, he was not so willing to help her make use of her new credentials. He agreed that her achievement was notable, but he felt she was overstepping her place. He argued that a job as a salesclerk was good enough and that she should aspire for no more that that.

Maud had to secure herself a job. To get a job, she needed to take interviews with prospective employers, but her grandfather was steadfast in his refusal to assist. Alexander would neither take her to interviews nor lend her a horse so she could reach them on her own. It left Maud with no other alternatives than to apply for positions she could reach by train or to make her presentation in writing.

Her success on both counts was abysmal. She was about to give in to what seemed to be the failure predicted by her grandfather. But then, just four days before the beginning of the school term in 1894, she was hired.

On a sweltering July 30, Maud screwed up her courage and put in her first day as an employed teacher. The experience facing her 20 pupils made her miserable. The job she had accepted took her to Bideford, just over 100 kilometres west of Cavendish, on the far side of Malpeque Bay. Only 19 years old, away from home, and completely on her own for the first time in her life, Maud was nervous, uncertain, and incredibly homesick. To top it off, she was boarding in the home of a Bideford minister who was a dour fellow she didn't like. She found it all quite overwhelming and cried for a week. But she stayed.

By August, enrolment in Maud's school was up to 38. In another month, it was 48. In her journal she noted that she had trouble with the students but even more with "those rotten old trustees" she had to placate. Still, she stayed through the winter. By June 1895, she had 60 pupils. Maud found a certain fulfilment in teaching and privately decided she would stay to teach in Bideford for another year.

All along, Maud continued to nurture her dream of

becoming a writer. *Ladies World Magazine* had accepted another of her poems for publication in the fall. During the winter, she religiously followed a writing regimen. She would get up at 6:00 a.m., dress by lamplight, and then, wrapped in a heavy coat, write for an hour with her Waverly pen clutched in her freezing fingers. She mailed her poems and stories to newspapers, magazines, and Sunday school papers — anywhere she thought they might be published. Her dedication, considering the conditions, was almost manic.

By the end of the school year, Maud had accumulated a thick stack of rejections but no new publishing credits. She carefully considered what might be the cause of her failure and decided she needed more education. Resolving to gain more classical training and a serious education in literature, she applied to Ladies College in Halifax. In response to the application, however, Maud encountered rejection of a different sort. The registrar told her she was too advanced for the college's curriculum. "You should apply to the bachelor of arts program at Dalhousie," she was told.

Dalhousie? The thought of applying to a university had never crossed Maud's mind. In the 1890s, female students at the highest post-secondary education levels were a rarity. Any who tried to assail the male-dominated system were considered interlopers. A woman was not to aim for professional training as a lawyer, engineer, or doctor. Women, in fact, were not considered intelligent enough to try. Canada's Election Act even seemed to support the contention. It classed women among such disenfranchised as idiots, lunatics, and criminals.

Considering the suggestion carefully, Maud asked herself, Why not? She was earning $130 a year and knew that, with some diligence and sacrifice, she could save a good portion of her tuition and living costs — she'd already managed to save all but $85. Having nowhere else to turn, Maud appealed once again to her grandparents. Predictably, her grandfather was absolutely against the idea. He wouldn't even consider the subject.

Maud resolved to wait him out one more time. Quitting her job in Bideford, she returned to Cavendish in 1895 and settled in at the Macneill homestead. She helped around the house, but devoted herself to writing. It was a frustrating period of more rejections but finally she succeeded. *Toronto's Ladies Journal* accepted her short story "A Baking of Gingersnaps." Cautious perhaps, or fearful of opening herself to more narrow-minded criticism in the village, she signed the story as Maud Cavendish. But her concerns were groundless because no one in Cavendish noticed the story.

Besides, Maud had received nothing in compensation from the magazine. In fact, in all the times she had sold her writing, she'd never been paid. With the most obscure publications, she did receive a complimentary subscription. On the odd occasion, she opened her mail to find a packet of seeds and a cursory note of thanks for her submission.

Maud did not let the rejections get her down though.

She had already decided it was a necessary part of her growth as a writer. "... [A]fter a while I got hardened to it and did not mind. I only set my teeth and said, 'I will succeed.' I believed in myself and struggled on alone, in secrecy and silence. I never told my ambitions and efforts and failures to any one. Down, deep down, under all discouragement and rebuff, I knew I would arrive someday."

She was just as determined to buck the odds and gain help from the Macneills. Her determination finally paid off when Lucy volunteered to pay for a year's tuition and housing.

In September 1895, Maud left home for a third time to enroll in a special course in English literature. She moved into Halifax Ladies College residence but quickly tired of that environment. The girls she was housed with were younger and shared few of her interests. Her outlook was more mature. Unlike the other students beginning their adulthood, she'd already thoughtfully considered plans for her future.

By December, Maud had found quarters of her own. In the privacy of her own room, she was able to devote herself to study and writing, which she did with the dedication of a professional. At 3:00 one morning, trying to come up with an entry for a contest in the *Halifax Evening Mail*, Maud dashed off a 32-line poem. Coincidentally, her English professor was the contest judge and, unbeknownst to him, he selected his student as the winner. The $5 prize was much needed, but Maud's head overcame her stomach. Though she could have used the money for essentials, she used every penny to buy volumes of her favourite poetry. Only a few days later, she received another $5 cheque — this one as payment for her story "Our Chivari" — from an American children's magazine called *Golden Days*. Not long after that, *Youth's Companion*, a magazine published in Boston, paid her $12 for her poem "Fisher Lassies."

In only a few weeks, Maud had moved from poverty to what she considered wealth. After all, at the time, she could buy a pair of boots for 95¢. "Never in my life, before or since, have I been so rich," she later wrote, remembering that time fondly. When her friends noticed her sudden riches, they expressed envy at such "easy" money. "I smile cynically," she scratched in her journal. "They do not realize how many disappointments come to one success. They ... think all must be smooth travelling."

Working herself too hard, Maud's health began to fail her again. First she suffered a bout of colds, then flu, and finally measles in November. Because measles was so dangerous, Maud was quarantined for a month in the Ladies College hospital. She missed enough of her classes to make passing the term impossible.

During her confinement, all Maud could think about was the end of the year and her chance to return to Cavendish for the holidays to visit friends and family. However, when she wrote home expressing that desire, she was bluntly told not to come. Her grandmother suggested the roads were too dangerous at that time of year to make the trip. Maud suspected another reason. "I know what that means," she wrote in her journal. "Grandfather doesn't want to be bothered meeting me or taking me back."

Lonely and discouraged, she spent the holiday season alone on campus. It was a preview of her inevitable departure from Dalhousie. By the end of the school year, Maud's funds had run out. Though she'd had success selling stories to several magazines, she needed more money. Knowing she would not receive additional support from the Macneills, and unwilling to borrow money from other relatives, Maud packed her things and went home, determined never to ask for help again.

Chapter 5
A Near Mistake of Passion

aud's return to Cavendish was fortuitous. Her second cousin Edwin Simpson had been teaching in Belmont, 65 kilometres away, but wanted to attend theological college. He offered Maud the chance to replenish her education kitty by taking on a temporary job as his substitute teacher.

Maud accepted immediately and then almost as quickly wished she hadn't. When she arrived, she found an uncongenial village she called "a wretched little hole." Maud boarded with Mr. and Mrs. Simon Fraser, living in a room she described as little more than a cubbyhole.

Very little about the Fraser household was worthy of compliment in Maud's opinion. She fell just short of criticizing the Frasers' daughter Laura, but not so for the rest of the family. She found Laura's brother Dan unattractive. Mrs. Fraser was an old, half-blind crone who rifled through Maud's belongings while she was away at school. Simon and Dan were so dirty and aromatic, she didn't even want to eat at the same table with them. The house was rickety and so poorly built the snow blew in during the winter — another winter Maud spent retiring into bed in her clothes, often unable to get any sleep at all.

She decided the pupils at Belmont were no better than her company in the Frasers' home, even impossible to teach. To give herself some comfort, Maud began attending revival meetings just to play the organ. She also started visiting with her second cousins, the Simpsons. The Simpsons had two sons, Fulton and Alfred, both of whom discovered an immediate passion for Maud.

In maturity, Maud had become a willowy beauty. Her grey-blue eyes, framed by long lashes, gave her an unintentionally flirty look. She arranged her long hair to cover her high forehead, which in turn accentuated her cheekbones. She was often a vivacious tease, mixing sarcasm with humour that men mistook as being coquettish. The Simpson boys were beside themselves, competing for the chance to drive her to church, fighting over who would have the chance to sit with her during the service. They came to blows over Maud on more than one occasion.

Amid her Belmont ordeal, and faced with the prospect

of fighting off two men she didn't particularly admire or want, Maud was surprised to receive a letter from Edwin. She had first met Edwin in 1892, when he was attending school in French River, near Cavendish. At that time, she'd decided he was too conceited to be a prospect for romance. Even so, she considered him attractive and, by reaching out to her in a medium she loved, Edwin improved in her memory.

Maud began corresponding with Edwin, sharing news about Belmont. By Edwin's fourth letter, it was obvious he was more than mildly attracted to her. On the fifth page of that long letter, Edwin confessed his love.

Sitting alone in her small room in the Fraser home, Maud began to think of Edwin a great deal. In her estimation, he might not make a bad husband, were he to become a professional of some sort. "Other men have loved me and I have always guessed it long before they told me but it never entered my mind that Edwin Simpson cared anything for me ... I might learn to care for him. He is a handsome fellow, clever and educated; our tastes in many respects are similar, and if I cared for him it would be a very suitable arrangement."

In reply to Edwin's love letter, Maud carefully let him know that though she felt no love for him then, if he was willing to wait and hope that she would one day feel differently, he might do so.

A response arrived in person in June 1897, when Maud was back in Cavendish for a visit. Edwin appeared as a guest speaker to the Sunday school class. "It will not be hard to care for him," Maud admitted to herself. But, aside from a few "violent fancies," Maud didn't think herself capable of falling in love. She also wasn't sure if she wanted to if that meant giving up her dream of becoming a writer. However, knowing what was waiting for her in places like Belmont and, at 22, also beginning to harbour fears of spinsterhood, Maud decided that should Edwin ask for her hand in marriage, she would say yes.

After one prayer meeting, Edwin volunteered to walk Maud home. She strolled with him, tense and expectant.

"I suppose you were surprised to receive that letter of mine last winter," he said.

It was all Maud needed. "I think I do care for you," she stammered in reply. "I will be your wife."

Maud allowed Edwin to seal his proposal with a kiss. Both agreed to keep their engagement to themselves and not set a date until after Edwin had graduated. Curiously, Maud found she felt relieved by this decision. Her unease at that observation grew as the hours passed. By that evening, she realized she had made a rash mistake.

Saying she would marry Edwin "marked the boundary between two lives for me ... the girl before that time was as dead as if the sod were heaped over her ... I am not Maud Montgomery at all. I feel as if I must have sprung suddenly into existence and she were an altogether different person who lived long ago and had nothing at all in common with this new me. I have been an utter, complete, wretched little fool. I see it all now plainly, when it is too late."

Having agreed to accompany Edwin to a sailing party the day after his proposal, Maud found herself watching him, listening to him. What she saw repelled her. In her eyes, Edwin had not changed from the conceited young man she'd met five years earlier. When he kissed her, she felt no passion. "I shrank away from his embrace and kiss. I was literally terrified at the repulsion which quivered in every nerve of me at his touch."

Over the next nine days of Edwin's visit, Maud refused to allow him to touch her. She felt caged. She couldn't bring herself to act as his lover, and Edwin was too busy talking about himself to notice. She came to dread the sight of him and wanted out of their marriage contract but didn't know how to make that happen. She was afraid to tell him, worried about how he would react. The emotional turmoil immediately affected her health. She couldn't sleep and developed dark circles under her eyes. She lost weight. The torment lasted the rest of that summer.

When the school year began, Maud accepted another position organized by Edwin. This time, she substituted for his friend Alpheus Leard in Lower Bedeque. While she worked there, she wrote and sold a few stories, but her heart was not in the process. Edwin was on her mind — so was the young son living in the home where she was boarding.

The Leards owned a prosperous farm in Bedeque, and 26-year-old Herman gave Maud the shivers. Herman was a strapping, muscular farmer with dark hair, blue eyes, and long silky lashes. Maud melted each time she gazed into those "magnetic blue eyes" and then felt a terrible wave of guilt for allowing herself the feeling.

For three weeks the couple joked and teased whenever they met in the house, gradually becoming more comfortable with each other. When Herman politely asked if Maud would care to take a buggy ride with him one night, her answer was obvious and instant. They chatted easily for hours. On their return, Herman put his arm around Maud, pulling her close enough for her to rest her head on his shoulder.

For Maud, who was still battling with her demon of an unwanted marriage to Edwin, the moment was pure joy. She confided in her journal that she felt "rapture such as I had never in all my life experienced or imagined." The following night, after a party the couple attended in a nearby village, Herman pulled her toward him again, this time pressing his cheek gently against hers.

Over the next few days, their encounters in the house were electric. Maud could barely function without her thoughts flitting to the last time she had felt Herman's cheek against hers. When, on their next buggy ride, Herman pressed his lips to hers in a soft, lingering kiss, Maud was thrilled. It staggered her to feel such an overpowering physical attraction, and she admonished herself to put an end to their encounters. Herman, she told herself "was not worthy to tie [Edwin's] shoelace." He had "no trace of intellect, culture or education."

Maud considered her life and her age at 23. A year of bliss with Herman, she reasoned, would be traded for a life of boredom. She resolutely determined to put an end to the budding relationship.

However, a few evenings later, Maud found herself sharing the parlour with Herman. She was writing a poem — though she found it nearly impossible to concentrate — and Herman was reading a novel on the sofa.

"My eyes hurt," he told her with mock fatigue. "Will you read it to me?"

Recognizing the request as a facile attempt to initiate conversation, Maud agreed anyway. Seated on the sofa next to him, she read to him. But she had barely begun before he was softly kissing her. Soon the gentle caresses turned into an embrace.

Although she was still haunted by her indiscretion, Maud could not bring herself to turn from Herman. Each night they met in the dark house until Christmas, when Edwin arrived for a visit. She visited with Edwin but was unable to voice her true feelings and her wish to call off the engagement. Some time after, she described her unease. "There was I under the same roof with two men, one of whom I loved and could never marry, the other whom I had promised to marry but could never love! What I suffered that night between horror, shame and dread can never be told."

Not brave enough to call off the marriage, Maud continued to meet secretly with Herman. At New Year's, she resolved to break it off once and for all with both men. She tried to avoid Herman in the close quarters of the house, but the temptation was simply too much. Maud knew that Herman wanted to consummate their relationship — she could barely resist "the most horrible temptation" herself when Herman visited her bedroom.

Despite her New Year's resolution, their liaison continued for months. Later, in her journal, she described just how deeply she felt for Herman. "I loved Herman Leard madly and, though I knew perfectly well I should be bitterly sorry the next day, his mere presence there brought me such unutterable happiness, so intense and passionate and all-pervading, that I could not thrust it from me at the command of conscience."

Maud confided that she was completely taken by her love for him and that she had to fight all her urges to give in to that attraction when they were alone in the Leard house. "I had never dreamed that I was capable of such love as possessed me — ay *possessed* is the right word. Simply to be under the same roof with him brought a strange torturing sweetness that nothing could wholly embitter — a blow from him would have been sweeter than any other man's fondest caress. Oh, Herman, Herman, you will never, never, never know how I have loved you!"

Maud's angst was interrupted when, on March 6, 1898, Alexander Macneill died from an apparent heart attack. When Maud learned of her grandfather's death, she seems to have exhibited an almost uncharacteristic lack of emotion. She certainly didn't evidence deep sadness at the news. "I cannot say that I have ever had a very deep affection for grandfather Macneill. I have always been afraid of him ... nevertheless, one cannot live all one's life with people and not have a certain love for them ..."

After attending the funeral in Cavendish, Maud began to realize her feelings for Herman were stronger than ever, returning "to gnaw and sting and burn." She was having trouble sleeping and stopped eating. She knew deep down that Herman was not the man with whom to share her life, but she couldn't stop loving him. She was "frantic with longing for his face." She couldn't write, couldn't function. In desperation, Maud even began to pray. "I will conquer," she wrote in her journal. "I will live it down even if my heart is forever crushed in the struggle."

Trying to resolve the conflicts she felt in her personality, Maud underwent some self-analysis. "I have a very uncomfortable blend in my makeup — the passionate Montgomery blood and the Puritan Macneill conscience. Neither is strong enough to wholly control the other." Maud debated herself internally and eventually resolved that no matter how fearful she was of Edwin's reaction, she had to put an end to their engagement. Rather than risk a face-to-face altercation with him, she took up her pen and delivered her bad news in writing.

Edwin, much to her chagrin, refused to accept her

retraction. Pleading his love, he begged her to give the decision more time, asking her to wait for three years and the
completion of his studies before making it a final refusal.
If, after that, she still felt the same, he agreed to accept
her decision.

It was too much for Maud to handle. In a fury, she wrote
again, this time filling her letter with nasty sarcasm. Edwin
reluctantly returned a photo she had given him — a sign of
his defeat.

Relieved about Edwin, Maud slowly tried to pull her
life together and regain the ground she felt she'd lost in her
writing. In her journal, she vowed to do whatever she must to
overcome her desire for Herman.

By October 1898, Maud felt she was ready to call her
love for Herman a faded memory. Deciding to test herself,
she travelled to Lower Bedeque. Instead of feeling indifference toward Herman, however, she found the same pas-
sions rising just at the sight of him. Frightened over what
might happen if she found herself alone with Herman, Maud
avoided him for the rest of her stay. With feigned disinterest,
she left Lower Bedeque, her heart aching.

Chapter 6
A Taste of Things to Come

In addition to her love life, Alexander Macneill's death brought an abrupt end to Maud's teaching career. In his will, he'd left his farm to his second son, John. Maud's grandmother was allowed to remain in the house until her death so long as she could maintain it. In the disposition of property at the turn of the century, this type of direction was common. Surviving wives, it seems, went with the furniture.

Maud had faced her uncle's scorn and ill will as a child. She knew that, were he given the slightest chance, her grandmother would be homeless and soon dead for the sake of her grandfather's arable land. And, as was customary for the last child left at home, Maud was expected to take care of her surviving grandparent.

When Alexander died, Lucy Macneill was 75, irascible, arthritic, and possibly going senile. To give up her teaching career was a tremendous sacrifice for Maud, but she felt she had no choice. Her world narrowed in focus to daily chores, her garden, and her writing. However, it didn't seem to bother Maud. "How I love my work," she wrote. "I seem to grow more and more wrapped up in it as the days pass. Nearly everything I think or do or say is subordinated to a desire to improve my work."

Maud selflessly cared for Lucy and, with just as much dedication, devoted her free time to her writing. She attempted to maintain a civil and friendly relationship with her uncle, as well. But as time passed, John was obviously becoming increasingly frustrated at not being able to assume the title to the homestead. In turn, John's reluctance to help Maud maintain the farm or pay for her grandmother's care was becoming a major frustration for Maud.

In 1899, Maud was hit by a death that made her question her decisions. Herman had died in June at the age of 28. Still holding his memory dear, Maud was shaken by the news and spent the night sitting by her window weeping. She'd turned from love and now regretted her decision. She confided in her journal that all she wanted at that moment was to be with Herman forever in his "unending dreamless sleep."

In January 1900, Maud got a small financial reprieve— along with some sad news. She received a blunt telegram from her stepmother informing her that her father had died in Prince Albert. "Hugh J. Montgomery died today. Pneumonia. Peacefully happy and painless death." To Maud's surprise, the father who had rarely supported her while alive had bequeathed her $200.

With $100 she had saved from teaching and the money she'd earned from writing, Maud's entire fortune could fit in a sugar tin. She was facing the future with the thinnest of margins for error but it didn't discourage her. She wrote in her journal that she had "a belief in my power to succeed. As long as I possess that I shall face the future with an unquailing heart."

Her bravado, however, soon leeched away. Three months after her father died, Maud told her journal that she had earned only $96.88 in 1899 from writing. Editors were still rejecting 9 out of 10 of her manuscripts.

For the next year and a half, she produced a flurry of submissions and became well enough recognized by editors to be offered a job. In September 1901, Maud was offered a position as a substitute proofreader for the *Halifax Morning Chronicle and Daily Echo*. The offer was a way to satisfy both her desire to move on and her Uncle John's to move in.

Maud understood that John intended to turn the homestead over to his son Prescott, who was impatiently waiting for an opportunity to get married — he needed a place to claim for his wife. So she proposed a compromise. She would take the job in Halifax. Prescott would assume caregiving duties of

Lucy. This way, Maud would have a chance to prepare for the inevitable when Lucy died and she'd be left homeless. Both parties agreed, and Maud accepted the job.

Once again, Maud moved to Halifax. The job paid a paltry $5 a week, but Maud felt the position gave her a foot in the door to becoming a full-time journalist. It also afforded her plenty of free time to continue her creative writing.

During the next nine months, Maud sold more than 30 stories. She needed to sell them to survive and offered no apologies for writing what she called "pot boilers." "I don't care much for writing such, but they offer good price for it." She told a friend: "I am frankly in literature to make my living out of it. My prose sells and so I write it, although I prefer writing verse. I know that I can never be a really great writer. My aspiration is limited to this — I want to be a good workman in my chosen profession. I cannot be one of the masters but I hope to attain to a recognized position among the workers of my time."

As well as proofing at the newspaper, Maud wrote a column called "Around the Table" that was signed "Cynthia" from October 1901 through May 1902. The column covered whatever took her fancy — including politics, astrology, astronomy, even photography. In effect, Lucy Maud Montgomery was operating successfully as one of Canada's first freelance writers. The creative side of her work earned her $500 that year.

Maud's future seemed finally to have settled onto a

writing path, but in the summer of 1902, Cavendish problems recalled her to PEI. Prescott informed her he could no longer put up with Lucy. He demanded that Maud stay in Cavendish. Maud understood completely why Prescott had flown from the homestead — Lucy was crippled with rheumatism and had become an even grouchier crone who was almost impossible to abide. However, out of the sense of duty that guided Maud in everything, she agreed to stay.

Lucy's final years were stagnating for Maud. She grew more and more unhappy with her duty each passing month. To occupy her time, she played the organ at church choir practices, but she hated it. The only social venue she had in Cavendish was the Literary Society, and she attended that only to borrow books.

Maud felt penned in by her responsibilities. The burden of caring for Lucy without the help of her aunt and uncle was draining Maud to the point of emotional bankruptcy. Life seemed poised against her. She even began developing irrational fears. She confessed in her journal to being afraid of the dark. The wind. She took to hiding from other villagers and pacing alone in her room. Memories of her past mistakes began to torture her. Maud's life, it seemed to her depressed mind, was over before it had really begun.

Then, quite by surprise, a small spark of interest was kindled in her dark thoughts when a handsome new face appeared in Cavendish in September 1903. At 33, Reverend Ewen Macdonald was a handsome, virile-looking man. His good looks were enough to entice more than a few appraising glances from Maud, the church organist. Ewen had a thick head of black hair matched by dark, roguish eyes, a pleasant smile, and a charming Gaelic accent.

While she thought him attractive enough, Maud maintained a lukewarm relationship with the new minister. She didn't want to encourage his friendship beyond pleasant social chat for fear a relationship might impinge on her writing career. Anything but superficial friendship could lead nowhere while her grandmother was alive anyway, she decided.

Maud began to suffer from nervous headaches, which were not at all helped by the intrusion of "poor old Grandma's set ways of age and rapidly increasing childishness." When Ewen began to make regular visits to the Macneill homestead to pick up mail, however, her attitude slowly improved. Ewen was something to look forward to every day. If there was no mail to be collected, he would spend time with Maud in casual conversation until another resident appeared at the door looking for correspondence. If Maud was busy with her postmistress duties, Ewen would mope on a bench outside, waiting patiently for his chance to see her.

As the months passed, Maud began to think she had more in common with the good-natured minister than she first suspected. She acknowledged in her journal that she was growing to like him. Though Ewen's conversation rarely strayed from general topics, Maud sensed his blossoming fondness. She decided, one more time, that if he asked, she would accept. "After all, this is a practical world and marriage must share in its practicalities. If two people have a mutual affection for each other, don't bore each other, and are reasonably well mated in point of age and social position, I think their prospects of happiness together would be excellent if some of the highest up-flashings of the 'flame divine' are missing."

However, Ewen lacked any affinity for Maud when it came to her creative side. And while she was coping with her domestic responsibilities, she was also struggling to establish her literary career. Happily, Maud found sounding boards elsewhere. In 1902, she'd started correspondences with Ephraim Weber in Alberta and then, in 1903, with George B. MacMillan in Scotland. Ephraim was a rancher who taught off and on and had been struggling to get published as well. George was a journalist.

Maud thought of George as a kindred spirit. They encouraged each other, and Maud was able to bolster her enthusiasm for writing by having the chance to "talk" to another writer on a personal level. They even traded samples of their work.

With George, Maud felt free to have animated discussions about literature, the possibility of life after death, reincarnation, morals, fairies — even herself. She once wrote this about herself to him: "Apart from my literary bent, I am small, said to be very vivacious, and am fond of fun and good times generally. I am interested in many things and love living. I have a camera and enjoy taking photos ... I love fancy work, CATS, horses, pretty dresses and feminine things generally. Revel in books. Don't go in for athletes but love out-of-doors."

In her exchanges with George, Maud displayed a feeling of freedom without the necessity of "conventional disguises." They indicate an odd dichotomy. She told him she'd been able to well disguise her true feelings in public. "I learned to meet other people on their own ground since there seemed to be no meeting place on mine ... I found that it was useless to look for kindred souls in the multitude."

While being careful to keep her public face separate from her private face, Maud continued juggling her passion for writing, her obligations to her grandmother, and her growing affection for Ewen.

But life took on a new lustre in 1905.

For several years, Maud had been keeping a notebook of ideas she hoped to someday expand into stories. That spring, that's exactly what she did.

"Elderly couple apply to orphan asylum for a boy. By mistake a girl is sent to them."

Anne "flashed into my fancy already christened, even to the all important 'e,'" she later described. "Soon seemed very real to me and took possession of me to an unusual extent."

Chapter 7
Anne Shirley Is Born

Maud wrote *Anne of Green Gables* during the summer of 1905.

What had begun as an idea for a short serial for a girls' magazine rapidly ballooned into more. Afraid she'd be mocked if the Cavendish locals knew she was writing a novel and it didn't get published, Maud kept her project a secret. She slept only five or six hours a night so she could reserve two hours for writing in longhand. When the book was finally finished, she tried to assess it objectively and decided it "wasn't half bad."

Maud mailed the manuscript to publishers with the same professional distancing she'd maintained with her other writing. She'd learned it was not worth the anguish to stew over whether something would be accepted for publication. After mailing her writing, she would begin something new as quickly as possible. When a manuscript was rejected, she didn't lose sleep. She simply mailed it out again.

While this approach worked well enough for short articles, a novel did bring with it an extra dash of hope. Gradually, the rejections Maud received for *Anne* left her little hope that it would ever be published. When the fifth and final publisher replied with harsh criticism, Maud decided to give up. The publisher's rejection had, after all, told her she was wasting her time: "Our reader has found some merit in it, but not enough to warrant publication." Reluctantly, Maud decided *Anne of Green Gables* wasn't as good a book as she'd thought and stuffed the pages in an old hatbox to be forgotten.

During the writing process, Maud had put a relationship with Ewen on hold. Now she began to wonder if that had been a good decision. He seemed no closer to proposing. Maud had started imagining what Ewen might say when he actually got the courage to propose. She waited patiently for him to act.

It took him until the autumn of 1906. On a rainy afternoon, he popped the question in an oblique way: "There is one thing that would make me perfectly happy," he told her. "It is that you share my life ... be my wife." It wasn't the romantic kind of appeal she might have hoped for, but Maud took it for what it was worth — a sincere proposal.

Maud told Ewen she wanted to accept but could not

until she was free of her grandmother. Ewen was the soul of understanding. He explained that he intended to quit his ministry in Cavendish so he could continue graduate studies in theology at the University of Glasgow. To him, a delay was perfectly acceptable.

Like they were brokering a sale, Maud and Ewen agreed to the terms of their secret engagement and Maud felt satisfied. But once Ewen had left for Scotland, Maud realized she missed him. His visits to the farm had been the highlights of her day. Without his smiles and jokes, Maud realized how important Ewen had become to her. She didn't consider Ewen intellectual, but she recognized "a certain depth of thought and feeling that was generally hidden and repressed, partly by his natural reserve." Over time, she found "more in him than I expected" and "began to be attracted by the man himself ... I was glad to see him — felt the loneliness of my life more keenly when he was away."

Maud's journal during Ewen's absence was filled with frantic accounts of her blackest moods. She suffered an attack of depression and neurasthenia, characterized by general weariness, irritability, lack of concentration, worry, and hypochondria. The condition spiralled into a complete nervous breakdown.

In Glasgow meanwhile, Ewen was depressed as well. He was in fact approaching a state of being dysfunctional because of an extended bout of insomnia. It had happened to him before, once in childhood and when he was at college in Halifax. A general feeling of malaise and melancholy seemed to be overtaking him. In April 1907, recognizing the deepening level of severe depression he was approaching, Ewen decided to give up on graduate studies and return to Cavendish and Maud.

With Ewen back, Maud began to feel even more restricted by her responsibilities toward Lucy. She was ready to move on and get married but still couldn't. By the end of 1907, she recorded a feeling of "great and awful weariness ... coupled with a heavy dread of the future — any future ... [t]o be happy would require more effort, more buoyancy than I shall possess."

Money had also become a pressing problem for her. When she was casting about for a subject she could use to craft a story that might sell, Maud remembered the *Anne* novel. She decided that if she could reduce it to seven chapters and send it out as a short story to a Sunday school paper, she might earn a much-needed $35 paycheque. She pulled it from the hatbox, ready to slash it. On rereading the manuscript, however, Maud felt it deserved one more chance, so she sent it out one last time — to L. C. Page Company in Boston.

Like a miracle, the manuscript was bought. At first, Page wanted to buy all the rights to the novel, but Maud had heard some disturbing accounts of Page's business ethics and refused. Instead, a 10 percent royalty was established. To gain it, Maud had to commit to providing Page with any other novels or creative fiction she wrote for the next five years. This seemed a reasonable enough request for a publisher to make of a first-time novelist, so Maud agreed. Page was delighted and immediately suggested she begin a sequel. Maud happily charged forward to write *Anne of Avonlea.*

Ephraim was the first to learn of Maud's success. On May 2, 1908, she wrote him: "I am blatantly pleased and proud and happy and I shan't make any pretense of not being so ... Don't stick up your ears now, imagining that the great Canadian novel has been written at last. It is merely a juvenilish story, ostensibly for girls."

It was a modest description given how important that book was to Maud. In her journal, she was more honest. "The dream dreamed years ago at that old brown desk in school has come true at last after years of toil and struggle. And the realization is sweet, almost as sweet as the dream."

When *Anne of Green Gables* was released to the public, the response to its warm and funny story was instant. It was launched in June 1908, and before the end of August, it had received 66 book reviews. The *Montreal Star* proclaimed it the "most fascinating book of the season." Within the next five months, it was reprinted six times.

Maud, who had been writing in obscurity for years, suddenly had fans. Mark Twain sent her a letter describing Anne as "the dearest, and most loveable child in fiction since the immortal Alice."

With the success being received by her novel, Maud was

gaining notoriety in Cavendish. That also brought her unaccustomed wealth — her first royalty cheque was $1730 — and with it some inconvenience. In August, tourists were already travelling to Cavendish to meet her. "I don't want to be met," she told Ephraim. She also resented her private life being exposed in the newspapers. She was weary, feeling sick, and had lost her appetite.

Worse, with the notoriety, she discovered unexpected jealousies among her relatives and friends. Only three months after *Anne of Green Gables* had been published, she wrote to Ephraim to complain. "A certain class of people will take it as a personal insult to themselves, will belittle you and your accomplishment in every way and will go out of their way to make sure that you are informed of their opinions."

Some readers said they wanted even more detail in the descriptions she had already presented in vivid detail. This riled Maud. As a reader, she resented "having too many images formed for me. I don't want too much description of anything or too many details in any description." On another occasion, she wrote, "When I read a story, I see people doing things in a certain setting; when I write a story I am the people myself and live their experiences."

Nonetheless, *Anne of Avonlea* was published in 1909. In 1910, just two years after her first publication, Maud received $7000 in royalties, an enormous sum for a writer — the average annual income for a worker in PEI at the time was just $300. But she was worried about the publisher's pressure to feed the reader frenzy. "If the thing takes," she wrote to Ephraim, "they'll want me to write her through college. The idea makes me sick ... If I'm to be dragged at Anne's chariot wheels the rest of my life, I'll bitterly repent having 'created' her.

"I'm Anne's slave already. The idea makes me sick. I feel like the magician in the eastern story who became the slave to the jinn he had himself conjured out of a bottle."

Maud had no idea just how true those words would be.

Chapter 8
Matron Bride

For years, Maud had been living a life of drudgery. She had to maintain the homestead, be Lucy's nurse and companion, and perform the postal duties she and Lucy inherited from Alexander. As Lucy grew older and more senile, she was a grinding burden. When she passed away in March 1911 from pneumonia, the death was likely a welcome relief. Maud could finally begin to think of herself and prepare for a new future.

Within weeks, Maud's Uncle John had dismantled the house and given away or burned what remained of his parents' belongings. Just as she'd always expected, Maud and her cat Duffy were forced to move immediately, first into the

Cavendish manse and then to the Campbell home in Park Corner. Ewen, who'd been posted to minister to churches in Leaskdale and Zephyr in Ontario the previous year, arranged for a stand-in.

By July, the couple was finally able to marry. The ceremony was performed in one of Maud's favourite places, the front room of John Campbell's house. As a 36-year-old bride, Maud might have been considered matronly, but she was willing to accept any label that day. She had finally reached the point where her only obligations were to her writing career and the man she'd chosen to be her husband.

Maud's wedding day was an emotional watershed for other reasons, too. Recalling that day in her journal months later, on January 28, 1912, she explained why. The wedding had been small but flawless, with a very notable meal prepared by her cousin Frederika. "And I shall always think mournfully of that dinner — for I could not eat a morsel of it. In vain I tried to choke down a few mouthfuls. I could not...I had been feeling contented all the morning. I had gone through the ceremony and the congratulations unflustered and unregretful. And now, when it was all over and I found myself sitting there by my husband's side — *my husband!* — I felt a sudden horrible inrush of *rebellion* and *despair. I wanted to be free!* I felt like a prisoner — a hopeless prisoner. Something in me — something wild and free and untamed — something that Ewan [sic] had not tamed — could never tame — something that did not acknowledge him as master — rose up in one frantic protest against the fetters which bound me. At that moment if I could have torn the wedding ring from my finger and so freed myself I would have done it! But it was too late — and the realization that it was too late fell over me like a black cloud of wretchedness. I sat at that gay bridal feast, in my white veil and orange blossoms, beside the man I had married — and I was as unhappy as I had ever been in my life."

Somehow though, in spite of those feelings, Maud managed to hide her doubts from a glowing Ewen. Not wasting any time, the newlyweds left that afternoon for Montreal. There, they boarded the White Star liner *Megantic*, bound for Europe and a three-month honeymoon during which she also met George MacMillan. It was the last time Maud would leave what she had always considered her home in Cavendish and Park Corner.

When they returned to Canada, Maud was introduced to another life — that of a minister's wife. The couple moved to the manse of St. Paul's Presbyterian Church in Leaskdale to the cheers of waiting parishioners. The manse had no indoor plumbing, and Maud had to do her writing at the kitchen table at first, but she accepted the change in lifestyle.

Her new world was a hectic whirlwind of volunteerism and church activity. As the wife of the Leaskdale minister, Maud was expected to take an active role in providing guidance and counsel, and she did her best with both. She took her role as minister's wife seriously, noting that "... the minister's wife has a special opportunity for service which is a privilege and not a duty."

In Maud's case, however, that opportunity was often more duty than privilege. "I haven't time to savour life at all," she observed in her letters to the pen pals. In her journal she wrote of the return of her headaches and nervous spells and the disillusionments that simmered behind her controlled public face. She was also pregnant by this time and worried about giving birth to a healthy child.

In the heat of the Ontario summer in 1912, Maud experienced the joy of two "births." The first occurred on June 30, when the freshly printed copies of *Chronicles of Avonlea* arrived at the manse in Leaskdale. A week later, on July 7, her first child, Chester, arrived. At 37, Lucy Maud Montgomery was finally a mother.

By late 1913, Maud was pregnant again. Sadly her tough pregnancy resulted in the stillborn birth on August 13, 1914, of Hugh, named after her father though never christened. The baby had apparently been healthy, but during the delivery, there was a problem with the umbilical cord.

The couple's third attempt at a child resulted in the birth of Ewan Stuart on October 7, 1915. Throughout that pregnancy, Maud showed signs of being anxious and depressed and would wring her hands and pray, "If only the baby will live!" Stuart was born healthy but, unlike his gregarious older brother, was a quiet boy, more studious than Chester.

As the boys grew up, Maud applied a flavour of the

stern upbringing she'd received with the Macneills. However, instead of a sharp tongue ready to demean the boys into submission, Maud used a more conventional spanking switch. The black stick was always handy, and Maud applied it as liberally as necessary.

Maud's years as her grandmother's caregiver had also made her a detail-oriented employer. She used her royalties to pay for a maid to do cooking and housework. Making daily lists of chores to be done, she would inspect the maid's work often. For the $22 a month plus board she paid, Maud demanded only the best effort. A second-rate job was unacceptable. When she found fault, the woman was told to correct and how, in no uncertain terms. Maud expected the staff to be respectful and demanded that the women she hired maintain a cheerful attitude at all times.

Not surprisingly, everyone in the family had the habit of reading at the dinner table. Maud read voraciously, often finishing one or two detective novels a day. She would also sit at the dinner table with her notebook. Her work schedule usually entailed writing in the living room from nine until noon. In the afternoon, she could be heard whispering and talking to herself as she reread her daily pages out loud. At night, Maud either wrote, did her scrapbooks, or jotted in her journal by kerosene lamplight.

By this time, World War I was on, and Maud took her volunteerism very seriously. She filled "every available chink and cranny of time" sewing and knitting for the Red Cross and serving as the president of the local branch. She was so involved in the news of war that she began to dream about the battlefields and came to believe some of the dreams were prophetic warnings. In one, a soldier rushed into the manse for shelter, upon which the sky cleared and Maud found herself crowned with flowers — spiritual proof, she felt, that her Red Cross work was worthwhile. She believed that on other occasions she had dreamed of the attack on Romania and battles in Belgium. Every crisis in the news gave her another sleepless night.

During this period, Ewen had again started showing signs of his mental illness and had ostensibly withdrawn from family responsibilities. Maud, helpless to do anything for him, felt like a single parent. As she struggled with her own family's problems, she was busy in the community consoling Leaskdale parents who had lost sons to the war.

The close contact with those grieving mothers and fathers may have aggravated Maud's sensitivity to the atrocities of the time. She began to worry herself into a frenzy over news of any battles. She scoured maps of Belgium and France, studying the reported movement of men and machines on the front lines. The ugly reality of the war hit her directly when her half-brother Carl arrived home after fighting at Vimy Ridge, missing one leg.

To find escape from Ewen's depression and the pall of grief that surrounded everyone in Leaskdale, Maud travelled to Cavendish for visits. To her, PEI, and her childhood coun-

Reverend Ewen MacDonald, 1917.

tryside, was a sanctuary — a place to recharge herself emotionally. "Oh, I felt that I belonged there — that I had done some violence to my soul when I left it."

In 1918, Maud visited PEI for six weeks. On holidays, she was free to be herself. She was down-to-earth, funny, and warm. She always wore an apron and carried a little notebook in her pocket to jot down ideas, memories. She practised speedwriting and was very fast with her notes. She loved walking and exploring — Lover's Lane was her favourite spot.

But, while Maud would return to PEI to renew her spirit, that happiness made her apprehensive. "The gods do not give such gifts out of mere wantonness of giving. They are meant as consolation prizes for the dark days to follow," she once wrote after a visit. This pessimism was perhaps deeply grounded by the way she'd been raised, by the disappointments and the resentments she remembered. Maud's past can be said to have shaped her core beliefs about herself and the world around her.

While the parishioners in Leaskdale were proud to have a famous author living in their midst, none took it for granted that Maud would interrupt her thoughts if they met her on the street. As Maud became more focussed on her novels, she seemed to pass into another world. She would often quietly whisper to herself until she was satisfied the phrases were in character and exactly right. If she happened to be strolling in Leaskdale at such a time and was greeted by a parishioner, there was no guarantee she would respond. After a few years of such conduct, parishioners took it as normal to hear "muttering" sounds from behind her closed door in the manse. To them, Maud was both special and eccentric.

Maud also set herself apart by the way she dressed — impeccably, just a notch above the average person. Yet those who knew Maud didn't take her penchant for wearing hats and stylish dresses as a sign of snobbishness. It was simply her way. Most people felt she was approachable and friendly most of the time.

Even Maud's dislike for fan adulation changed over time. She grew to enjoy the attention. Feeling an obligation to thank anyone who took the time to compliment her writing, Maud made a point of answering every fan letter with a handwritten note. In some cases, a reply might take a long time if she was working on a book project, but Maud eventually wrote back. With a flourish that was unique to her, she often signed her correspondence by including a small sketch of a cat with her name.

But the Leaskdale parishioners' assessments of Maud were only partly right. She was really never a mixer. She confided to her pen pals that she hated the word and had been forced to become a mixer, or at least "an excellent imitator of one" in the role of minister's wife. "What agonies I have endured betimes when I was dying to laugh but dared not because I was the minister's wife."

While Maud was a pious Christian, her beliefs didn't quite fit with the parishioners'. Since she was a child, she'd expressed her closeness with the divine through her appreciation of nature. She thought of the trees and flowers as individuals capable of feeling and with feelings of their own. It was hardly a philosophy one might expect from a minister's wife.

Maud once wrote to George, "I call myself a Christian in that I believe in Christ's teachings and do my poor best to live up to them." She also told George that though she attended and helped with church services, she didn't feel comfortable with group prayer. "I don't remember public prayers as necessary. I don't care for any kind of public prayers, not even in church. These are nearly always farces, and generally unpleasing farces."

Instead, she took spiritual inspiration from the outdoors. "If I really wanted to pray ... I'd go out into a great big field all alone or into the deep, deep woods, and I'd look up into the sky ... into that lovely blue sky that looks as if there was no end to its blueness. And then I'd just ... *feel* a prayer."

And while the parishioners in Leaskdale may not have sensed this dichotomy in Maud, her family certainly felt its effects. Stuart once described his mother's dual nature as: "She was extremely sensitive, although an excellent dissembler, and though she experienced great peaks, she also fell to great depths emotionally, which does not make for tranquility. This rigidity and sensitivity prevented any easy camaraderie in the family, but she was capable of inspiring deep affection in all of us."

When her contractual commitment to L. C. Page was satisfied, Maud had sought a more compatible publisher, settling on the Canadian firm McClelland, Goodchild & Stewart (now McClelland & Stewart).

This decision began a 10-year legal battle with Page. The difficulties began when Page did not pay $1000 in royalties Maud claimed was owed her and argued it had the right to continue to produce reprints. Following the advice of her new publisher, Maud joined the American Authors' League. Through that organization, she secured the legal assistance she needed to pursue Page in the U.S. courts.

However, Maud was only partly successful. She won the $1000 but lost in her declaration that Page had no permission to produce reprints. Maud, upset with the ruling and distracted by the pressure of dealing with Ewen's illness, probably accepted poor legal advice just to settle the issue with Page. She sold Page all rights to the books it had already published. The sum Page paid to Maud in settlement appeared to represent a legal and moral victory, but it was a false one. No sooner had Page paid her the $18,000 negotiated than it sold the first motion picture rights to her books for $40,000.

Maud's first two books with McClelland, Goodchild & Stewart, *Anne's House of Dreams* and *Rainbow Valley*, were published in 1917 and 1919, respectively. *Rainbow Valley* had taken Maud more than a year to write. Following the war, however, she was able to resume a more manageable writing schedule. During the winter of 1919, she copied her diary over into journals with the intent of giving a copy to each of her boys. She also began writing *Rilla of Ingleside*, using the war years entries in her journal as grist.

Once *Rilla* was complete, Maud hoped "to say farewell

to Anne forever." After writing another book about "that detestable Anne," she told her pen pals she was "sick of her and wonder that the public isn't too." *Rilla*, she said, was to be "positively the last of the Anne series. I have gone completely 'stale' on Anne and *must* get a new heroine. Six books are enough to write about any girl."

During the writing of *Rilla*, Ewen had a mental collapse and fell into a deep depression. He perceived himself to be in a kind of torment, damned to suffer eternal punishment, but he was unable to provide any particular reason why he felt this way. It may have stemmed from the Presbyterian tenets of predestination — the belief that some people are predestined to an afterlife in hell regardless of their saintly conduct. But understanding the possible cause didn't help Maud cope.

In an attempt to find treatment for Ewen, she took him to a Boston nerve specialist. He was prescribed chloral, a drug that smoothed mood swings, and then admitted to a sanatorium. He returned to Leaskdale five weeks later. In November, Ewen suffered a relapse and Maud discovered new problems with Page. The Boston company had decided to publish *Further Chronicles of Avonlea* from short stories Maud had penned during the term of her contract.

Although Maud had strictly forbidden Page from using anything in the book's promotion that might lead readers to believe the book was about Anne Shirley, Page connived to put a red-haired girl on the cover, implying that this was an Anne book. Maud acted to have an injunction served to stop Page, but the company published the book anyway. She responded to the Page publication with another lawsuit. In her journal, she sadly dated 1919 as an end to her happiness. It was almost a prophecy.

In July 1920, Maud returned to Leaskdale from a trip concerning the suit to once again find Ewen miserable. Her life seemed to have become an unending battle against foes she could not overcome.

Chapter 9
Failed Directions

Maud was fed up with how her life had become so entwined with that of her fictional heroine. She finished writing *Rilla of Ingleside* in August 1920 and wrote to Ephraim Weber that it was indeed to be the last Anne book. "I am done with Anne forever — I swear it as a dark and deadly vow. I want to create a new heroine now — she is already in embryo in my mind. Her name is Emily."

As if trying to exorcise the ghost of Anne Shirley from her imagination, Maud began to write *Emily of New Moon* in 1921. It took her only six months to complete, the shortest time she'd taken to write any novel. Comparing Emily's fictional life to Maud's, parallels are obvious. Maud used to write letters to her dead mother, and Emily writes letters to her dead father. Maud also used Emily's life to recount how her own desire to be an author had been sneered at by those who mattered to her.

While Maud may have found a kindred spirit in her fictional creation, she was feeling increasingly lonely in the real world. Ewen's melancholy episodes had him withdrawing further from any emotional intimacy she may have been able to share with him. In her journal, she confessed to never loving her husband with the same passion she had once felt for Herman. Maud described her unhappiness and her acceptance of it. "The last thirteen years of my life [in PEI] were certainly not happy years, and parts of them were violently unhappy. Yet there were many hours of happiness and sweetness in them, too, — the happiness of a loved work and success in that work, the happiness of wonderful communions with sea and field and wood — and I tasted this happiness again in writing over those years.

She added: "Perfect happiness I have never had — never will have. Yet there have been, after all many wonderful and exquisite hours in my life."

Yet she continued with her usual steely core of discipline, showing a smiling face in public. She explained Ewen's absences as bouts of headaches, intimating a physical cause for them rather than a mental malady. Like a skilled actress, she played the role of contented minister's wife to anyone who might inquire.

It was in her journal and letters to pen pals that Maud exposed her real feelings. "Happy? With my heart wrung as it is! With a constant ache of loneliness in my being! With no one to help me guide and train and control my sons! With my husband at that very moment lying on his bed, gazing at the ceiling and worrying over having committed the unpardonable sin!"

With each book Maud wrote, her fame grew, but the public adulation did nothing to erase the pain of her private life. Still, Maud realized she had to maintain momentum for her books. So, although she wished to do nothing more than disappear back to PEI, Maud regularly travelled across the country giving talks to women's groups.

In 1923, her achievements were recognized by the Royal Society of Arts in England, and she was invited to become Fellow of the Society. In accepting the honour, Lucy Maud Montgomery became the first Canadian woman to be so recognized.

The pleasure of that award seemed to spur Maud to attempt a new direction in her career. Nearing 50, she had been characterized as an author of books for young women for almost 20 years. This assessment may have troubled her. Maud's talent was recognized by both her peers and her reading audience, but perhaps her ego and pride were prodding her to prove she had as much to offer as an author of novels for adults. To that end, Maud crafted an adult romance she titled *The Blue Castle*, which was published in 1926.

She dedicated it to Ephraim.

Maud had by this time witnessed a seriously troubling decline in Ewen's mental health. Ostensibly a single parent, she had also begun facing new challenges with her sons. Chester was particularly worrisome. "There are some things about Chester that make me anxious in regard to his future," she wrote.

Chester had always shown a wild side. When he was six, visiting Silver Bush, he'd managed to start his parents' car and promptly drive it into a brook. As he reached his rebellious mid-teen years, Maud was finding it difficult to curb his gregarious nature. He spent much of his time pursuing girls. Maud may have feared that this would lead to unwanted outcomes. So she used some of her royalties to send him to St. Andrew's College in nearby Aurora, hopeful the discipline there might settle him.

In February, Ewen accepted an assignment to Norval, a small community about a half hour from Toronto. The previous year, many Presbyterian churches joined Methodists and Congregationalists to form the United Church of Canada. Ewen and Maud opposed that union and had succeeded in convincing two congregations to side with them.

Despite her private trials in Leaskdale, Maud had enjoyed the friendships she'd made and was sad to leave. "I am alone in the manse," she wrote on her last night in Leaskdale. "By this time tomorrow night everything will be gone. I am terribly tired but perhaps I will have a better sleep than the first night I slept here ... Sometimes I wander about the stripped rooms with my memories of vanished days. I have a very dreadful feeling of 'lostness' and emptiness as if all emotion were drained out of me and the resulting vacuum were more dreadful to bear than pain. Good-bye, old life. Tonight I forget your terrible hours and think only of your bright and pleasant ones."

In many ways, the move to Norval represented a fresh start. Even the manse, with such modern conveniences as plumbing and electricity, was an improvement. By the time of the move, Maud had written 14 books and was working on a 15th. *Emily's Quest*, the last of the series with her new heroine, was published in 1927.

Although her writing had sometimes been described as too descriptive and sentimental, Maud redeemed each novel by injecting her delicate sense of humour. Her stories sparkled. They were funny. For observant readers, Maud skillfully shaded a darker, subtler element in each plot. She explored issues of independence, courage, love, and bias.

In 1927, two other important occasions marked Maud's life. That summer, her long-time correspondent Ephraim Weber travelled to Ontario for a visit. So did someone else.

On August 27, a letter from British prime minister Stanley Baldwin made Maud realize that her skill with the pen crossed not only geographic borders but social ones. Baldwin was in Canada with the Prince of Wales and Prince George. He was requesting the opportunity to meet one of his favourite authors when the royal dignitaries visited Ottawa to mark Canada's 60th anniversary of nationhood. Maud, of course, happily accepted.

Maud continued to enjoy her celebrity for two years, but when Black Tuesday crumbled North America's financial underpinnings in October 1929, she felt the impact. The crash badly cut into her investments and made the frills in her life — a housekeeper and boarding school bills — difficult to maintain. The bills ate heavily into Ewen's salary.

Before cutting back, Maud attempted to collect on some personal loans. During her Leaskdale years, family and friends had often borrowed but had never, except in one instance, repaid. Maud, always sensitive to the needs of others, had even lent money to total strangers. Her debtors begged for time and the forgiveness of their obligations, and Maud relented on her collections, recouping very little of the money due to her.

Without any alternative, Maud was forced to rely on her writing income. It was the first time since she had been supporting herself and her grandmother in Cavendish that she needed royalties to contribute to her living expenses. Turning out saleable popular books therefore became a very serious pastime. To make matters worse, that year she suffered a three-week bout of influenza. Barely recovered from that, she fell down the stairs and sprained her arm, which took seven weeks to heal.

By 1930, Maud's worries had grown considerably. "I

worry over many things," she wrote, "some of them the kind that can't be told to the world but must be hidden and not spoken of." Ewen's health was a constant concern. She felt the pressure of producing books to pay for expenses. Her promotional mind worked overtime thinking of ways to maintain interest in her books.

In October, Maud headed west on a speaking tour. She used the journey to reacquaint herself with Laura Pritchard Agnew and Ephraim Weber. Soon afterward, her energy renewed by the adulation she received on the tour, Maud began a novel she decided to call *A Tangled Web*.

Chester, in the meantime, had managed to graduate high school and was enrolled in engineering at the University of Toronto. Still, Maud eyed her eldest son warily. He'd been showing serious interest in his girlfriend, Luella Reid. She didn't want him to marry until he could support a family. Though Maud encouraged Chester, his first year of university was a scholastic disaster, and he failed. He followed that with news that he'd been fired from a mine job in Sudbury that was supposed to help pay for his schooling.

Just 56, Maud showed evidence of feeling old. In a letter to George MacMillan in March 1931, she complained, "I say to myself 'I believe in a series of re-incarnations.' If that is true I am really nearing the time when I will be young again." By the end of that year, Maud's stress manifested itself with physical illness, and she suffered another bout of neurasthenia. The condition incapacitated her. Because her stress was worse the next year, and worse again the year after that, time did not easily heal.

In the midst of writing *Pat of Silver Bush*, Maud felt the need to renew herself emotionally and physically. She decided on an extended vacation on her beloved Island, and uncharacteristically during a month-long fall visit, didn't turn to her journal.

When she returned to Norval she was in a more positive frame of mind, but quickly had to acknowledge being away hadn't dissipated her troubles. Soon after she finished her latest novel, Maud learned that Chester had been asked to withdraw from his mine engineering classes at university. Apparently he had failed most of his Christmas examinations and one professor claimed Chester failed to attend classes.

Rather than give up on their son's future, Maud and Ewen redoubled their efforts to encourage stability in his habits. They helped Chester study so he could get work in a law office as a prelude to attending law school — having given up on expecting him to try to pass his first year of engineering for a third time.

Their effort seemed to pay off. Chester claimed he liked law. In addition, Stuart was the junior gymnastic champ of Ontario and then the national champ in 1933. That May, at 17, Stuart enrolled in medical school. In her letters, Maud expressed delight with what appeared to be a positive turn of events in her life.

Her happy outlook was quickly smothered. She learned

that Stuart was apparently playing cards in the residence common room too much and overindulging in sports. She worried that he might make the same mistakes his brother had.

On January 15, 1934, Maud began writing a sequel to *Pat of Silver Bush*. Her journal entries showed that life had become desperately difficult. Halfway through his first year of law school, Chester sheepishly announced he had defied Maud's wishes about having a serious relationship with Luella. Though he spent the week living with his parents and attending school, on weekends he'd been sneaking away to see Luella for trysts at her parents' home. Because of Maud's attitude, Chester had felt forced to keep the relationship secret until it was no longer possible. Out of necessity, Chester told his mother, he had married Luella. He was to be a father.

The news stupefied Maud. Not only had Chester flagrantly disobeyed her, he'd covertly maintained two separate lives. Nevertheless, with grandmotherly joy, Maud opened her heart to her first grandchild, Luella Agnes Josephine Macdonald, born on May 17, 1934.

All Maud's fears for Chester were realized by the bundle she soon held in her arms. Stoically, she accepted this turn of events. Though she was anguished by it all, she agreed to set the newlyweds up in a Toronto apartment — with a warning. She would support them only if Chester promised not to sire more children until he finished law school.

Around the same time, Ewen suffered another debilitating bout of melancholy. On June 11, Maud wrote that he was receiving "electric head treatments" and was on several pills, none of which seemed to help. His escalating insomnia finally contributed to a complete nervous breakdown. Beyond her ability to care for her husband, even with a housekeeper's help, Maud resorted to outside care, committing him to the Homewood Sanatorium in Guelph.

Maud tried to use Ewen's time away to recuperate herself, but her journal entries got progressively darker throughout the summer. Ewen was released in August, but he had to rest at home for two more months, requiring Maud's constant care. By September, her journal entries were practically a nurse's logbook of Ewen's condition. He "groaned and maundered," "cried; heard voices." Maud wrote he was "cranky and hateful," that he complained of "feeling like falling" and had a "crazy conviction that he is 'forbidden to preach.'"

On September 4, she described almost feeling revulsion for him during his bleak depression states. "Eleven. Ewan [sic] has brooded all this hour and will not talk. I made him take a glassful of Vip. He looks terrible — sullen, unshaved, vindictive. The change in Ewan's appearance during these spells is almost unbelievable. Normally, he is a fine looking man, with clear-cut features and friendly dimples. But in these spells he seems almost bestial — hideous. I can't bear to look at him. Nobody has ever seen him in one of them — I have always been able to prevent that. They could never forget it."

That fall, Ewen nearly died, not from his ailments but from his treatment. His doctors had prescribed a regimen of mood-stabilizing drugs, which he was given religiously, until an inattentive pharmacist accidentally dispensed the wrong pills. In combination with his other drugs, Ewen was poisoned by the incorrect pills. Only through swift medical attention, was he pulled from death. Maud's response was to move him to PEI, where, after another month in bed, he recuperated.

Back in Norval, the bitterly cold winter beat Maud down. It was so unlike how, in the early years, she had written prolifically in spite of wintry conditions. Maud said that besides his physical ailments, Ewen suffered from what she termed "religious melancholia." She continued to do her best to disguise his mental state from his parishioners.

Ewen's delicate condition persisted, however, so Maud sent him to Florida to recuperate. She stayed in Norval to be near the boys and began writing *Mistress Pat*. But her progress on the novel was arduous. Maud suffered through cold after cold and fought a constant losing battle to stay warm. Nonetheless, she was able to buckle down and spent her 60th birthday struggling to complete the book's final chapter. Except for the company of an irritating, uncooperative maid, Maud was alone.

Maud wrote that 1934 was "quite the most terrible year I have ever lived." She looked hopefully forward to 1935 and the chance that her life might slip into a more manageable flow. Ewen had recovered enough to return to his duties as a minister, Chester appeared as though he would abide by her rules and study to become a provider for his young family, and by all accounts Stuart was diligently pursuing his educational goals as well.

However, Maud's teetering hopes soon toppled.

Chapter 10
Journey's End

arly in 1935, Ewen responded to a form letter from the church regarding arrears in his salary. It was to spell the end to his ministerial career.

Church officials mistook Ewen's response as a complaint, and the otherwise good relations the couple enjoyed with the church were badly tainted. Maud, who had been directing the church drama group, even writing plays for them, was ousted from her position. Ewen was granted a leave of absence. In February the church requested that he resign altogether.

At the same time, Maud learned that Chester had not turned over a new leaf at all. The law firm where he'd been articling had lost its patience over his lackadaisical work habits and summarily dismissed him.

Amidst the rush of packing to leave Norval, Maud described her feelings about the sorry combination of new disasters. "I have been a mouse in the claws of destiny. For a few moments now and then she leaves me alone — just long enough for a little hope of escape to rise in my heart."

Finding a new place to live was the next hurdle. At first it appeared Maud and Ewen might not be able to afford to buy a home at all. However, on March 8, one of those moments of reprieve occurred and luck smiled in her direction. Maud found a quaint house on the banks of the Humber River in Toronto that she and Ewen could afford if they managed their money carefully.

At 60, Maud was excited about the prospect of moving into the first house of her own, a handsome pseudo Tudor that she named Journey's End in the hope she'd never need to move again. To make the down payment, Maud had to sell the last of her stock investments. She had truly become the sole breadwinner in the family — she and Ewen would be relying on her writing for income. If they were to survive, she could no longer experiment with adult novels. Maud knew she had no choice but to go back to proven formulas in her writing.

Pushed by this new urgency, the day after moving in, Maud found a place to compose among the shipping crates and began to write a new Anne book. She was under tremendous professional and creative pressure. Her memories of childhood that had given Anne Shirley such uniqueness were not as fresh. Worse, her venerable English publisher, Hodder and Stoughton, was concerned about a shift in reader appetite and had turned down *Mistress Pat.*

The bad news from England was followed by better news from France. On March 21, Maud learned she had been elected to the Literary and Artistic Institute of France. While pleasant, the news was small compensation for her disappointment regarding the first rejection she'd gotten since sending out *Anne of Green Gables* and the general dissatisfaction she felt about her life. "I wish the honour would cure my sciatica, banish neurasthenia and take away all the bruises of my soul and spirit," she wrote.

More accolades continued that year, helping to maintain Maud's popularity as a mainstream author and the book sales she so desperately needed. To the pride of her nation, Maud was also invested with the Order of the British Empire. For the prestigious occasion, Maud freshened her wardrobe and attended the ceremony at the Governor General's residence in Ottawa, the picture of stylish elegance — almost. Much to her amusement, Maud later discovered that as she had proceeded through the solemn ceremony with sombre seriousness, her slip was showing. For a woman who always prided herself on her appearance, it was a comical irony.

In the months that followed, emotional conflicts between Chester and Luella threatened to tear apart their

Despite commercial success, happiness
eluded Maud later in her life.

fragile marriage. After one spat, Luella packed up the baby
and fled to Norval to live with her widowed father. Even with
her financial problems and the ongoing burden of Ewen's
mental instability, Maud opened her home to the boys and
allocated a room to each — Chester because of his breakup
with Luella, and Stuart because he had failed his first year

of medicine at the University of Toronto and Maud perhaps felt he needed to be more removed from the distraction of dormitory life.

In 1936, Ottawa presented Maud with another surprise. She learned that the Canadian government was proposing a national park in PEI that would stretch along 40 kilometres of shoreline and be centered on Cavendish. The government planned to purchase property to preserve the land and the lanes so colourfully described in Maud's books.

Because the Macneills' farmhouse had been demolished years before, the government paid Keith Ernest Webb $6000 for his farm to serve as a stand-in and gave him a job as park warden on the property. The Webb home was then transformed with tremendous care and detail to look like Green Gables as described by Maud.

The honour must have been enormously fulfilling for Maud. But, like the other official recognitions she received, it did nothing to fix her crippled private life. The constant emotional stress took its toll on Maud. Ewen was showing signs of memory loss and Luella was pregnant again. Worse, Chester, who was still living in Maud's house, had left his diary open in his room, and Maud read that he was having an adulterous affair.

In the face of all this, Maud suffered a nervous breakdown. For a year, her nervous prostration was so severe she didn't even confide in her journal. The silence signalled, probably more clearly than anything else, the desperate state of her outlook.

When she resumed her notes in her journal, her writing focused on Ewen. In July 1937, she wrote that Ewen "... talked to himself, couldn't remember how to dress himself and sat for days with hair bristling, blue underlip hanging down, eyes glaring, face livid ..."

Maud was unable to take up a pen and write fiction. Her life was just too disjointed. On September 12, 1938, a year since she had written a single line of creative work, she began *Anne of Ingleside*. For weeks she was blocked, unable to make any progress. On September 27, she confessed that she had "tried to write but had to give up and go to bed."

But the pressure was on and somehow Maud managed. In November she recorded that Ewen was barely in touch with reality, that he had spent a night orating nonsense with fantastic gesticulations. On December 28, amazingly, she finished her 24th book in four months of hard writing. It was published the following year.

With Maud's encouragement, her sons had continued at university and both graduated with their respective degrees. By 1939, Maud might have been able to settle into a quiet retirement with her cats — if she'd had a different family. In February, she recorded that Ewen was taking patent medicines and seeing a long line of doctors in a hypochondriac search to find a cure to his ailments. His hunt was a drain on their finances.

Chester too, having graduated with a law degree, was

looking for money to get himself settled into a law partnership. Using her only assets of any significance, Maud sold the cinematic rights for *Anne of Windy Poplars* and *Anne's House of Dreams*. With the money, she helped arrange Chester's partnership in an Aurora law office and watched thankfully as he reunited with Luella and his children.

Even so, the skies in Maud's life continued to hang over her in a grey pall. In mid-1940, Maud suffered another "dreadful nervous breakdown" after a bad fall. This coincided with the depressing news of World War II that Canada was receiving from Europe. As she had been during World War I, Maud was extremely concerned. In December, she noted the intolerable financial distress she was under. Bills were piling up, and there was no new novel in hand to furnish a fresh infusion of royalties.

Once again, Maud's black state of mind was evident in how little she penned in her journal or her personal correspondences. By 1941, her letter writing had dwindled to little more than postcards. When she did write more, it was deeply disturbed. "Oh God, such an end to life. Such suffering and wretchedness," she wrote in July. That year, Chester's law practice, started with high hopes and heavy investment by Maud, ended in financial loss and professional failure. Chester and Luella divorced soon after their son, Cameron, was born. Plus, to Maud's chagrin, Stuart was likely facing military service.

Maud's physical and mental health began to plunge.

Much of the time, she was bedridden and too weak to hold a pen. On December 23, 1941, she sent George MacMillan a postcard thanking him for his years of friendship. "This past year has been one of constant blows to me. My oldest son has made a mess of his life, and his wife has left him. My husband's nerves are worse than mine even," she wrote, ending with a final goodbye. "May God bless you and keep you for many years. There are few things in my life I have prized as much as your friendship and letters. Remember me as I used to be, not as I am now."

Three days later, Maud wrote a sobering and heart-breaking letter to Ephraim Weber. The extent of her mental and physical deterioration was evident in the words and the almost illegible handwriting. "My dear friend," she wrote. "A hypo enables me to hold a pen for a few moments. Thanks for your book. I will read it if I ever am able to read again. I am no better and have had so many many blows this year. I am quite hopeless."

Lucy Maud Montgomery died on April 24, 1942. Twenty years earlier, always the planner, she had selected her burial plot in Cavendish. She felt the site was destined for her. "There, sometime I shall lie and the wind will creep up from the sea to sing over me and the old gulf will croon me a lullaby ..." At last she was buried on her hill to the gentle brush of that Cavendish wind.

Epilogue

There is no question that Lucy Maud Montgomery and her most famous character, Anne with an "e," were successful. Even so, during her lifetime, Maud often oscillated between great pride for having created Anne Shirley and her story to dark moments of artistic regret.

The Anne books were a mixed blessing for Maud. While her prolific output helped her maintain financial freedom, the demand for more of the same hobbled her as a writer. Though she tried to break free of Anne by writing for adults, the sad circumstances of Maud's life never allowed her the time or opportunity.

Maud presented a public version of herself and performed that role, in character, with brilliant skill. She was Lucy Maud Montgomery — respected writer. To the world, there was nothing more that needed to be said. She never marred her brilliant literary accomplishments by exposing her personal demons. Had she done so, perhaps the world would have recognized her other great strengths — her devotion to family, strength of character, intellectual insight, feminist opinion, and spiritual nature.

It is a sad irony that a writer who brought so much happiness to readers the world over lived such a troubled life.

Appendix 1
The Life of Anne and Friends

Lucy Maud Montgomery's "hatbox book," written with wit, humour, and joy, survives as one of the greatest works in Canadian literature. *Anne of Green Gables* is available in 32 editions and has been celebrated on stage and film. It has even been presented as a musical with record-breaking longevity in Canada.

From the moment she was given life in book form, Anne Shirley has represented the essence of independence. She's been a model of wit and courage for young women the world over. The freckle-faced redhead is now practically as recognizably Canadian as the maple leaf.

Anne first appeared on the motion picture screen as a "silent" version of herself in 1919, depicted by Mary Miles Minter. The young orphan's character so captivated Mary that her fiction overshadowed the actress's reality. In hopes of cashing in on the popularity of the feisty island girl, Mary legally changed her name to Anne Shirley. However, Mary was Anne Shirley in name only, and she soon disappeared into obscurity, along with the film.

When Maud viewed that 1919 film, she reportedly

fumed. To her, the Minter rendition of Anne was false and spiked for audiences like a sweet punch at a party. Story elements that Maud did not approve had been added, which also angered the author.

Thirteen years later, Maud didn't like the "talkie" version of her book much better. But in an article she wrote for *Chatelaine* magazine, she at least conceded that the actress portraying Anne had "tricked even me into feeling that she was Anne" on several occasions.

To Maud's relief, the Anne Shirley she imagined survived in spite of Hollywood. For the next 30 years, Anne lived only in the words Maud had written. Then, in 1965, decades after Maud's death, *Anne of Green Gables* emerged in yet another form. This time as a musical staged at the Confederation Centre of the Arts in Charlottetown. Within four years, critics in London were calling the production the best new musical of the year. *Anne of Green Gables — The Musical* is now a perennial favourite in PEI and has been performed in schools by amateur thespians across Canada.

In 1970, the production moved across the globe and was staged in Tokyo, with the Tokyo Philharmonic providing the score. Since then, thousands of Japanese have flocked to PEI to experience the charm of Maud's birthplace for themselves. The island of Hokkaido is even home to a theme park that is a careful reconstruction of Anne's world.

With the success of the musical, it was not long before Anne moved on to television screens. The television movie debuted in December 1985 to national acclaim and was then broadcast as a miniseries on PBS. When the movie went into international circulation, it was an incredible hit in Australia and England and appeared to good reviews in both Germany and Scandinavia.

Industry awards followed. The production won nine Gemini awards, Canada's television awards. Anne suddenly experienced a new burst of appeal. A sequel went into production in 1987. After it aired, Anne Shirley became big business in PEI as tourism to the province spiked. *Anne of Green Gables* holds the record as the Canadian miniseries with the highest average audience — 5.6 million viewers, or more than 15 percent of Canada's population.

But the fans wanted still more Anne. In 1990, *Road to Avonlea* debuted on Canadian television. One in 10 Canadians watched. It was unheard of for a story already so well covered to have maintained the same enthusiastic fan base, but the figments of Maud's imagination kept the entire country enrapt.

In its first season, *Road to Avonlea* devoted 13 episodes to parts of Maud's books and stories, including *The Story Girl, The Golden Road, Chronicles of Avonlea,* and *Further Chronicles of Avonlea.* By the second and third seasons, very little was plucked from Maud's written work.

It made no difference to the audience. The characters, those same engaging folks they'd met in Maud's stories, kept them tuned in. The national television audience adored them

Anne in front of Green Gables, portrayed by Jenna MacMillian,
a singer and dancer and popular Anne impersonator.

and their quirky lives and forgave the literary blasphemy of the scriptwriters. The fans wanted the show to run indefinitely. But after the seventh season, the producer had had enough, worrying that the stories would start to get stale.

Road to Avonlea was viewed in more than 100 countries and also won numerous awards. In Canada, it barely lost viewership from the astounding debut to its final episode. When that aired in March 1996, more than 2 million Canadians watched.

Two years after the series ended, another production company determined it was time to reprise the "Maud Montgomery Mania" in Canadians, and *Emily of New Moon* debuted. The series was an emotion-charged antithesis to the sugary themes of the Anne stories. It presented what the producers called "harsh reality." While this series too was successful, it fell short of the success achieved by *Road to Avonlea*. Still, *Emily of New Moon* prompted a new crop of readers to seek out more of Maud's yarns. Book sales for her first novels climbed as a result.

The television productions have spawned other elements of Maud mania. In 1993, an annual Lucy Maud Montgomery Festival was created in Cavendish. The festival is now one of the top 100 events in North America, according to the American Bus Association. That same year, the Uxbridge town council purchased the St. Paul's Presbyterian manse that Maud and Ewen called home from 1911 to 1926 and proclaimed it a heritage site. There are museums dedicated to Maud and her works in Norval and Bala, the Muskoka area that inspired Maud when she penned *The Blue Castle*. Maud mania has even inspired Anne Shirley lookalike contests!

The fan base for Anne continues to grow, and the L.M. Montgomery Institute, forged in 1993 to preserve and protect the author's memory, has seen it expand around the world. In June 2004, Japan's Princess Takamado was named the institute's International Patron. This honour acknowledges the millions of Japanese who have embraced *Anne of*

Green Gables since the book's translation into Japanese in 1952. Canada's Anne Shirley has truly joined the pantheon of literature's greatest characters.

Appendix 2
Books by
L. M. Montgomery

Anne of Green Gables, 1908

Anne of Avonlea, 1909

Kilmeny of the Orchard, 1910

The Story Girl, 1911

Chronicles of Avonlea, 1912

The Golden Road, 1913

Anne of the Island, 1915

The Watchman and Other Poems, 1916

Anne's House of Dreams, 1917

Rainbow Valley, 1919

Further Chronicles of Avonlea, 1920

Rilla of Ingleside, 1920

Emily of New Moon, 1923

Emily Climbs, 1925

The Blue Castle, 1926

Emily's Quest, 1927

Magic for Marigold, 1929

A Tangled Web, 1931

Pat of Silver Bush, 1933

Mistress Pat, 1935
Anne of Windy Poplars, 1936
Jane of Lantern Hill, 1937
Anne of Ingleside, 1939

Appendix 3
Lucy Maud Montgomery's Life At a Glance

1874	Born November 30
1876	Mother dies
1890	Travels to Prince Albert to be with her father
1891	Returns to Cavendish
1893	Attends Prince of Wales College and earns a teacher's licence
1894	Teaches in Bideford
1895	Attends Dalhousie University
1896	Teaches in Belmont
1897	Becomes engaged to Edwin Simpson; teaches in Lower Bedeque
1898	Returns to live with Grandmother Macneill when Grandfather Macneill dies; breaks engagement to Edwin
1898	Herman Leard dies

1898	Father dies
1901	Works at *Daily Echo* in Halifax
1906	Secretly becomes engaged to Ewen Macdonald
1908	*Anne of Green Gables* is published
1911	Grandmother Macneill dies; marries Ewen
1912	Chester Cameron born
1914	Hugh Alexander dies at birth
1915	Ewan Stuart born
1923	Becomes first Canadian woman named a Fellow of the Royal Society of Arts in England
1926	Moves to Norval
1927	Presented to Prince of Wales and Prince George
1935	Moves to Toronto; elected to Literary and Artistic Institute of France; made an Officer of the Order of the British Empire
1936	Cavendish chosen as site for national park
1942	Dies April 24
1943	Ewen dies

Bibliography

Bolger, Francis W. P. *The Years Before Anne.* 2nd ed. Halifax, Nova Scotia: Nimbus Publishing. 1991.

Bolger, Francis W. P., and Elizabeth R. Epperly. *My Dear Mr. M: Letters to G. B. MacMillan.* Toronto, Ontario: McGraw-Hill Ryerson Limited, 1980.

Bruce, Harry. *The Life of L. M. Montgomery.* Toronto, Ontario: Seal Bantam Books, 1992.

Gillen, Mollie. *Lucy Maud Montgomery.* Don Mills, Ontario: Fitzhenry and Whiteside, 1978.

Gillen, Mollie. *The Wheel of Things.* Don Mills, Ontario: Fitzhenry and Whiteside, 1975.

Heilbron, Alexandra. *Remembering Lucy Maud Montgomery.* Toronto, Ontario: The Dundurn Group, 2001.

Lunn, Janet. *Maud's House of Dreams.* Toronto, Ontario: Doubleday Canada, 2002.

McCabe, Kevin. *The Lucy Maud Montgomery Album*. Toronto, Ontario: Fitzhenry and Whiteside, 1999.

Rootland, Nancy. *The Sacred Sites of L. M. Montgomery*. Halifax, Nova Scotia: Nimbus Publishing, 1996.

Rubio, Mary, and Elizabeth Waterston. *The Selected Journals of L.M. Montgomery — Volume IV*. Toronto, Ontario: Oxford University Press, 1998.

Rubio, Mary, and Elizabeth Waterston. *Writing a Life: L. M. Montgomery*. Oakville, Ontario: ECW Press, 1995.

Rubio, Mary, and Elizabeth Waterston. *The Selected Journals of L. M. Montgomery — Volume III*. Toronto, Ontario: Oxford University Press, 1992.

Rubio, Mary, and Elizabeth Waterston. *The Selected Journals of L. M. Montgomery — Volume II*. Toronto, Ontario: Oxford University Press, 1987.

About the Author

Stan Sauerwein lives and writes in Westbank, British Columbia. A freelance writer for two decades, Stan has written articles that have appeared in a variety of Canadian and U.S. magazines and newspapers. Specializing in business subjects, he has written for both corporations and governments. He is the author of six other books — *Rattenbury: The Life and Tragic End of B.C.'s Greatest Architect, Ma Murray: The Story of Canada's Crusty Queen of Publishing, Klondike Joe Boyle: Heroic Adventures from Gold Fields to Battlefields, Moe Norman: The Canadian Golfing Legend with the Perfect Swing, Pierre Elliott Trudeau: The Fascinating Life of Canada's Most Flamboyant Prime Minister*, and *Fintry: Lives, Loves and Dreams*.

Acknowledgments

The author would like to acknowledge the incredible resource of history compiled by the L.M. Montgomery Institute.

Quotations from the *Selected Journals of L. M. Montgomery, Volumes I, II, III, and IV* © 1985, 1987, 1992, 1998, University of Guelph, edited by Mary Rubio and Elizabeth Waterston, and published by Oxford University Press Canada, are reproduced with the permission of Mary Rubio, Elizabeth Waterston and the University of Guelph, courtesy of the L. M. Montgomery Collection Archival and Special Collections, University of Guelph Library.

Quotations from the unpublished journals of L. M. Montgomery © University of Guelph, are reproduced here courtesy of the L. M. Montgomery Collection Archival and Special Collections, University of Guelph Library.

All other material written by L. M. Montgomery is reproduced here with the permission of David Macdonald, trustee, and Ruth Macdonald, who are the heirs of L. M. Montgomery.

Photo Credits

OTHER AMAZING STORIES

These titles are available wherever you buy books. If you have trouble finding the book you want, call the Altitude order desk at 1-800-957-6888, e-mail your request to: orderdesk@altitudepublishing.com or visit our Web site at www.amazingstories.ca

New AMAZING STORIES titles are published every month.